Should I Sleep W

Should I Sleep With the Boss?

And 99 Other Questions about Having a Great Career

Dr Rob Yeung

CYAN

Copyright © 2008 Rob Yeung

First published in 2008 by:

Marshall Cavendish Limited
Fifth Floor
32–38 Saffron Hill
London EC1N 8FH
United Kingdom
T: +44 (0)20 7421 8120
F: +44 (0)20 7421 8121
E: sales@marshallcavendish.co.uk
www.marshallcavendish.co.uk

and

Cyan Communications Limited
5th Floor (Marshall Cavendish)
32–38 Saffron Hill
London EC1N 8FH
United Kingdom
T: +44 (0)20 7421 8145
F: +44 (0)20 7421 8146
E: sales@cyanbooks.com
www.cyanbooks.com

A CIP record for this book is available from the British Library

ISBN-13 978-0-462-09922-4
ISBN-10 0-462-09922-9

Designed and typeset by Curran Publishing Services, Norwich, UK

Printed and bound in Great Britain by
Mackays of Chatham, Chatham, Kent

Contents

Preface   *xi*

The Questions

1. What does it take to get to the top?   3

2. What's the best way to get a pay rise?   5

3. What's the best way to get promoted?   7

4. Why should I care about organizational culture?   9

5. What are the secret rules everyone must learn to
    get ahead?   11

6. How can I figure out what my company keeps secret
    from me?   13

7. How do I get headhunted?   15

8. What's the best way to ask for a pay rise?   17

9. To what extent should I speak my mind at work?   19

10. Why am I not happier in my work?   21

11. Should I fake enthusiasm at work?   23

12. Do I need a career plan?   25

13. How can I stop or avoid drifting in my career? 27

14. So how can I create my personal vision? 29

15. I'm struggling – what aspects of my life should a vision cover? 31

16. What are the pitfalls involved in writing a personal vision? 33

17. What's the best way to set effective goals? 35

18. How can I figure out whether to accept a new job offer? 37

19. Should I bother hiring a professional coach? 39

20. Should I get involved with office politics? 41

21. What are the essential rules of office politics? 43

22. How can I develop my political savvy? 45

23. How can I get colleagues to agree to my plans? 47

24. How can I escape the ranks of middle management? 49

25. Should I write goals down? 51

26. How can I manage my time better and become more productive? 52

27. Why should I focus on *important* rather than *urgent* tasks? 55

28. So what does effective time management look like in practice? 58

29. How can I create an interruption-free zone at work? 60

30. How can I tame the paperwork monster? 62

31. How much socializing do I have to do with my work "buddies"?   64

32. What's the best way to express complaints at work?   66

33. How much does appearance really matter at work?   68

34. Should I focus on my strengths or work on my weaknesses?   70

35. How can I manage my weaknesses?   72

36. Why do I need to understand my signature strengths?   74

37. What are my signature strengths?   76

38. How else can I discover my signature strengths?   78

39. How can I progress quickly from the bottom rung of the career ladder?   80

40. How can I survive the dreaded annual appraisal?   83

41. Does anyone really listen to negative feedback?   85

42. What's the best way to get constructive feedback?   87

43. How can I deflect criticism?   89

44. How can I learn and develop myself?   91

45. How else can I accelerate my self-development?   93

46. What's the best way to deal with organizational change?   95

47. Why should I network?   98

48. What's the secret to effective networking?   100

49. What's the best way to kick off my networking campaign?   102

50. How can I deepen relationships within my network? 104

51. How can I extend my network? 106

52. Any final tips on effective networking? 108

53. How important is intelligence in determining career success? 110

54. What else could I do if I'm not classed as traditionally "intelligent"? 112

55. Do I need an MBA? 115

56. Does emotional intelligence really matter? 117

57. So how can I sharpen my emotional intelligence? 119

58. How can you change someone's behavior? 121

59. How can you repair a relationship that has broken down? 123

60. What's the best way to give constructive criticism? 125

61. How can I defuse conflict at work? 127

62. What is the best way to deal with *interpersonal* conflict? 129

63. How can I improve my popularity at work? 132

64. How can you offer praise without sounding insincere? 134

65. How can I improve my listening skills? 136

66. How can I deal with a difficult colleague? 138

67. What are the major differences in people's personalities? 140

68. Why don't people listen to me?   143

69. How can I be more influential?   145

70. How can I fend off an office bully?   147

71. How many hours a week do I need to work to
    succeed?   149

72. How can I improve my work–life balance?   151

73. How can I learn to say "no"?   153

74. What are different ways I can say "no"?   155

75. Do I need to build my profile at work?   157

76. How can I develop my profile and visibility at work?   159

77. Can jargon ever be a force for good?   161

78. What is good meeting etiquette these days?   163

79. Why am I bored with my job?   165

80. Is it possible to feel more passionate about my job?   167

81. How can I be happier in an existing job?   169

82. How can I find my calling in life?   172

83. What's the best way to explore new career options?   174

84. I want a new job – how can I write a great CV and
    pass interviews?   176

85. How can I achieve fulfillment in my working life?   178

86. How can I become an entrepreneur?   180

87. Do I really need a mentor?   182

88. How can I find my Yoda?   184

89. How can I solve (or avert) a mid-life (or quarter-life) crisis?   186

90. Are copying and stealing really good tactics for career success?   188

91. How can I manage my useless and/or bastard boss?   190

92. Should I sleep with the boss?   192

93. How can I keep up with the changing world?   194

94. So what's all this rubbish about having a personal brand?   196

95. How can I create or revamp my personal brand?   198

96. What's the best way to handle a crisis at work?   200

97. How can I develop my charisma and presence?   203

98. What's the difference between a manager and a leader?   205

99. How can I be a great leader?   207

100. Any final tips on creating a successful and fulfilling career?   209

About the Author – Dr Rob Yeung   *211*

Preface

What do you want from your work? Maybe you want to make it to the very top, to have the big salary, the corner office, and the recognition and respect for being the best at what you do. Perhaps you feel that you're not making the most of your talents and wonder what you could do to feel more fired-up at work. Or maybe you want to achieve more in less time at work so you can get on with the more enjoyable stuff in your life outside of work.

This book answers these questions – and more.

At work we are given targets and told to strive for them in order to help our organizations to meet their goals. But what about what you want? Let's not worry about what your employer tells you to do for your organization. Instead, let's think for a change about what you should do for yourself.

Consider what it is about your work that you would like to change, improve, or achieve. All of these topics (and more) are tackled in this book:

✓ A desire to climb the career ladder more quickly.

✓ Working for a bad or incompetent boss.

✓ A desire to be more influential, impactful, or inspiring at work.

✓ A feeling of uncertainty about your future career.

✓ Feeling under-appreciated by your employer.

✓ Wishing you could achieve more in less time.

✓ A lack of career progression.

✓ Unsatisfying relationships with colleagues.

✓ A sense that you lack career direction.

✓ Having to work long hours.

✓ Aspirations of setting up your own business.

✓ Doing work that you feel is not stimulating enough.

✓ Wanting to find your calling in life.

✓ A feeling that you're in the wrong job.

✓ High levels of stress at work (or in life).

✓ Wishing you could feel more motivated or happier in your work.

✓ A desire to improve your work–life balance.

✓ A sense that you may not have clear enough career goals.

✓ A feeling that you don't "fit" into your organization's culture.

✓ Feeling that your work is adversely affecting your personal life.

Any of that sound at all familiar? If so, read on. Because this book is about how to get more out of your working life. Whether you want to make grand changes or tackle specific issues at work, this book will help you to achieve your goals. So read on if you want to find answers to the questions that you have always wanted to ask. Read on to learn how to shape your work and career to become more successful – and happy too.

Dr Rob Yeung
rob@talentspace.co.uk

The
Questions

1 What does it take to get to the top?

It's hard to answer a question like this without sounding over-simplistic. But at the risk of reducing whole libraries-full of research and years of business thinking into only a single sentence, the secret is to understand that getting ahead at work is fundamentally about people.

Yes, people skills trump everything else. Nothing is more important – not analytical flair, technical know-how, planning and organizing skills, a knack for numbers, commercial savvy, creative talents. Unless you work alone in a sealed room with no contact with the outside world, you can only succeed by communicating with people and influencing them.

Whatever your goals, you must ultimately ask other people for resources such as their time, their patience, their enthusiasm, their willingness to take a chance, their understanding, their check books. And you can't force any of that from anyone. Success comes only from having great relationships in which people like you, trust you, and want to work with you and put opportunities your way. You can't compel a boss to give you interesting work or coerce a customer into buying from you; you can't demand that a colleague help you, or bully an investor into investing with you. Maybe you could get away with it once – but never again.

No matter how many reasons you can give to support your argument, no matter how bright or right you are, people can choose to do what they want. And (I've said it before but it's worth saying again) unless other people like you, trust you, and want to work with you, you will never succeed at work.

While all of this may seem painfully obvious to most of us, bear in mind that an astonishing number of people never learn to communicate effectively and work well with others. Get the relationships in place and the rest often falls into place. As such, much of what is contained within this book is to do with relationships, politics, networks, and people. In the old days, relationship building was called "interpersonal skills," but now it's called "emotional intelligence" (see Q57 on how to develop yours).

> # Getting ahead at work is fundamentally about people.

2 What's the best way to get a pay rise?

There's both good news and bad when it comes to boosting your salary. The good news is that you can earn more. The bad news is that you may have to quit your current organization and go to work elsewhere.

Employers have always been much better at paying market rates to attract new employees than paying anywhere near market rates to retain them. Once you have signed on the dotted line, your pay rises will almost certainly be limited by company rules – perhaps linked to the level of inflation or organization-wide pay deals. Rarely are such rules sufficiently flexible to recognize even the outstanding efforts of great employees. I know – it's tough on you and a bit short-sighted on the part of employers, but that's how the organizational cookie crumbles.

What that means is that if you want to earn more, the best way to get it is to find a new job. You will be ten times more likely to get a pay rise by switching organizations and moving into a slightly larger role or a better-paying sector than by simply asking for a pay rise where you currently work. If you are determined to ask for a pay rise from your current boss, see Q8 – but don't say that I didn't warn you. Because so long as you are wedded to an employer, your pay will only grow by tiny increments. Have you considered whether it's time to get divorced?

> # If you want to earn more, the best way to get it is to find a new job.

What's the best way to get promoted?

A promotion is yours for the taking if you can satisfy a couple of conditions. First, you need to be doing the "right" job – in other words a job that you are passionate about or at least can get reasonably motivated about doing. If you wake up and dread having to go to work or feel indifferent about it, you will never be able to work as hard or do as good a job as others who wake up and feel excited about it. If that's not you, then find something else to do (Q80), as you will struggle to get a promotion without divine intervention.

The second condition requires that there are promotions to be had. If the organization has a very flat hierarchy or is growing only slowly or not at all, you may be waiting for "dead men's shoes" – for a more senior person to quit, retire, or literally die before a vacancy becomes open – which could take a very, very long time. And how long are you prepared to wait for that opportunity to become free?

Assuming that you enjoy what you do and there are promotions to be had, the biggest piece of advice is to make sure you are noticed by communicating your value to the people who count. Being the "best" at a job is rarely enough to assure your ascent. Too many people are "good" at their jobs but get overlooked when it comes time for promotions to be handed out.

> # Be good *and* be noticed if you want to forge ahead.

Of course that's unfair, but the reality of organizational life is that performance at work is inherently subjective. If you work in sales you may be able to point to exactly how many units you sold and how much money you made. But practically no other job can be evaluated so objectively. Most people are measured on skills such as teamwork, creativity, communication, problem solving, or customer care – how can such skills be measured in a way that is not open to at least some element of interpretation?

Once you realize that there is a subjective element to all performance evaluations, you can't help but realize the need to communicate your successes to the people that count. Being better at a skill than a colleague is of precious little use unless the people at the top see you demonstrating the skill or at least hear about your good deeds.

Don't fall into the trap of trying only to be good at your job. Be good *and* be noticed if you want to forge ahead.

4 Why should I care about organizational culture?

Organizational culture is that set of implicit rules – a code of behavior or "the way things are done around here" – that determines how people behave towards each other at work. Read the culture right and your colleagues accept you as one of their own. Get the culture wrong and you stand out like an outsider, an interloper, a freak. Which wouldn't be so bad except that doing so could lead to clashes with colleagues and even raise questions about your future within the organization.

Often, a culture is set by the behavior and standards of the founders of an organization or by its senior management. Most people like people who are like themselves, so culture becomes self-propagating. The people at the top recruit and promote people who resemble themselves, and so the culture survives. It's all very tribal: if you do the same as your tribe, you survive; if you don't do what the other members of the tribe do, you could end up with a spear in your back. So be careful that your bosses do not end up having a conversation about you along the following lines:

"I can't put my finger on it, but I don't like _____."
Yes, that was your name in the blank.

Asking how or why the rules came into being are the wrong questions to focus on. There is rarely a good reason for them. Ask colleagues why they behave a certain way and they might say, "it's just the way it is" or "I don't know – we always have though." Ask instead how to abide by the rules.

Ignoring the unspoken rules of culture will cause unnecessary moments of friction with colleagues. Others may not even consciously realize why they don't like you; they will simply have a niggling feeling that you're doing something not quite right.

Obeying the rules won't help you to succeed if your work is of poor quality. But breaking them will make life that much tougher for you. Trust me when I say to look around you to understand the cultural norms within your organization (Q5) and ask the advice of a mentor too (Q87).

> # Get the culture wrong and you stand out like an outsider, an interloper, a freak.

5 What are the secret rules everyone must learn to get ahead?

Organizational cultures differ along a number of dimensions. Use these questions to uncover four of the key characteristics of your organization:

✓ *How direct are people allowed to be?* At one extreme, some organizations promote a culture in which people are permitted to be honest and forthright with each other, in getting straight to the point, sharing both bad news and good, and saying what they mean even if it might elsewhere be construed as bluntness. Other organizations (particularly those with their origins in the Far East) prefer that messages be couched in more tactful language, encouraging people to express messages implicitly rather than too directly.

✓ *To what extent is consensus expected?* Some organizations encourage debate from all members of the team. At its polar opposite, other organizations value consensus and unanimity, and may see more than a modicum of debate as unruly and disrespectful.

✓ *To what extent are employees controlled by the organization?* At one end of this continuum, certain organizations may have a hierarchical, top-down style of management in which employees must obey instructions and seek approval for even relatively small deviations from agreed plans. At the other end of the continuum of control, other organizations set very broad goals and encourage employees to be much more autonomous, risk taking, and to use whatever methods they see fit to achieve those goals.

✓ *How are people expected to work together?* All organizations claim that they foster teamwork. But sometimes the reality is that they actually promote individual stars with little regard for the overall performance of the team. Other organizations do not merely talk about the importance of teamwork but treat with contempt individuals who conduct themselves without considering the needs of the team.

Figure out where your organization sits along each continuum. Work out how you need to behave in order to survive and thrive.

6 How can I figure out what my company keeps secret from me?

You won't ever find the secret rules of your culture written down. But just because they are not captured in writing does not mean that they do not exist.

The secret rules of culture often contradict what an organization preaches in public. On paper the organization may say that "the customer is always right," but in practice the business may be doing everything it can to tell customers they're wrong in order to wriggle out of its responsibilities.

Look around you and observe the behavior of colleagues that you respect. Be mindful of what they *do* rather than what they *say*. But avoid simply copying what the senior managers do. There may be one rule for them and another rule for people lower down the organization such as you. Unless respected peers are also behaving in a similar fashion, be careful not to overstep any boundaries.

Study carefully also the evaluation and reward systems at work. If you identify the behaviors that get rewarded, you can understand not only *what* to deliver, but also *how* best to deliver it. In many organizations, the means are as important as the ends.

> # The secret rules of culture often contradict what the organization preaches in public.

Seek the opinions of a mentor (Q87) and watch out for pockets of culture across the organization too. The Hong Kong office may have its own twist on corporate culture from the New York or Frankfurt offices. The marketing folk may be more adventurous in their decision making than the finance folk – or even vice versa.

Look, listen, question, and learn. But here's a final word of warning: uncovering the cultural rules of your organization can teach you only how to blend in – it won't necessarily make you happy. Consider whether your organization's culture rubs up against your personal values. Can you put up with it, because that's what it takes to get ahead, even though it pains you on a daily basis? Or would you rather quit? Do what it takes or leave. The ultimate choice is yours.

7 How do I get headhunted?

There seem to be certain individuals who never need to apply for jobs. Bigger and better jobs just seem to come their way. But imagine if a stream of ever more exciting and challenging – and well-paid – jobs could come your way too. Here's how you can make it happen for you:

✓ *Be good at what you do.* First and foremost make sure you are respected for your work. Headhunters employ researchers to ring round and quiz people for recommendations, but you will only get recommended if you are at least halfway decent at your job. Specializing in a scarce skill is often a good way to get noticed too.

✓ *Raise your profile.* Present at conferences, speak at industry events, get quoted by journalists, and get published even if it's only in your internal company newsletter. Especially in the era of the Internet, providing even a one-line quote to a journalist (and making sure that the journalist spells your name correctly and mentions your job title and organization!) could be enough for you to appear on the radar of a headhunting firm somewhere.

✓ *Use the Internet.* Draw attention to yourself with your own website or a blog – although be careful not to write anything that could cause your employer to take offence. If you have the seniority, make sure your profile is on your company website too.

✓ *Network, network, network.* I've already mentioned that search firms employ researchers to help them identify possible candidates to fill their vacancies. The more people you tell about your skills and availability, the greater your chances of a researcher calling one of your contacts and being given your name (see Q49).

✓ *Initiate contact.* Research which firms are the most appropriate for job seekers with your experience and skills and send them your CV. No, it doesn't look desperate. But bear in mind that the top firms are often inundated with CVs all the time, so ask someone within your network to set up an introduction.

✓ *Maintain contact.* Make sure to pass your new contact details on to any executive search firms you have relationships with. Otherwise your successor may get the call, not you.

Draw attention to yourself.

---

8 What's the best way to ask for a pay rise?

I've already mentioned that the easiest way to earn more money is by swapping your current organization for a new one (Q2). However, if are determined to ask for a pay rise from your existing employer, make the most of your chances by following these steps:

1. *Research your case.* Contact recruitment consultants and other people within your external network (Q51) to find out how much people like you are getting paid elsewhere. But if you're already earning more than those elsewhere, you're probably not going to get a pay rise – so quit while you're ahead.

2. *Determine what you want versus what you need.* Experienced negotiators know they will rarely get what they initially ask for. Be clear in your mind as to what you would *ideally* like versus what you are *realistically* prepared to accept. Suppose you want a 10 percent pay hike, but would 8, 6, or 4 percent be tolerable?

3. *Assemble your argument.* Recall to mind occasions on which you made a contribution over and above those of other members of the team to cite as evidence of your greater value.

4. *Determine likely objections.* Your boss may say, "There isn't the budget," "Maybe we should wait until this time next year" and

so on. Brainstorm likely objections so you can prepare counterarguments to aid your case.

5. *Decide on the right time to approach your boss.* Timing is everything. Choose a moment soon after completing some exemplary piece of work.

6. *Keep the tone of discussion positive.* Demonstrate empathy with your boss's concerns through your word and body language. Be gentle in pursuing your argument and making your counterarguments. Even a hint of aggression or threat on your part will likely close down negotiations.

7. *Bear in mind there's more to your pay than mere salary.* If your boss can't give you a straight-up pay rise, how about a larger pension contribution, a guaranteed performance bonus, a shiny new laptop, an extra few days' annual leave, and so on?

Finally, if your boss says no to your request, ask exactly what you need to achieve to qualify for a pay rise in say three or six months. Pursue it politely but doggedly until you get it in writing. Then work like crazy to achieve your targets and claim your prize.

9 To what extent should I speak my mind at work?

Most managers say that they encourage debate. But what managers say is not always what they mean. Be careful to respect your organization's unwritten rules about speaking out around people who are senior to you. In answer to the question: by all means have an opinion, but be careful about expressing it.

The more junior you are, the less you may be expected to say. Every time you wish to open your mouth to speak, consider how welcome your comment may be. Would it be perceived as thought provoking or naïve? Providing a fresh perspective or exposing an uncomfortable truth?

Senior people do ask questions that appear on the surface to invite answers. However, self-important bosses often like to hear the sound of their own voices. Rhetorical questions from pompous bosses are not always meant to be answered. No one likes to be contradicted or told that they are wrong – especially when the person telling them is younger or less experienced.

If you feel strongly that you must disagree, do it on a one-to-one

> # Rhetorical questions from pompous bosses are not always meant to be answered.

basis. Preface your point of view with the possibility that you may have misunderstood the situation and you soften the blow. Even if you believe that a decision or action is possibly immoral, unethical, or illegal, be careful of saying so in public. There is an old adage that warns people to praise publicly, but criticize privately. Pointing out in front of others that someone is wrong or even disagreeing with them – especially someone more senior – is career-limiting stuff.

A useful guideline is to make your point no more than twice. If a senior person disagrees with you in spite of your repeated point of view, back down immediately and elegantly. Be watchful of your tone of voice and body language too, as sitting in silence with gritted teeth could appear as hostile as openly calling them an idiot.

Why am I not happier in my work?

I met someone the other day who could not be happier in his work. He never gets the "Monday morning feeling" about going to work or that "Friday feeling" about being free from it. When you meet someone like that, it's a bit nauseating, isn't it?

The reality for many people is that they could be happier in their work. And it typically comes down to some combination of three reasons:

✓ *A mismatch between your strengths and the daily demands of the job.* If you enjoy meeting customers but rarely get the chance, you're going to feel frustrated. If you hate numbers but your job requires you to crunch them for hours on end, time will pass exceedingly slowly for you. The more you get to use your talents on a day-to-day basis, the happier you will be. To find the right job for you, first discover your talents (Q37) then reshape your job and how you spend your time (Q80).

✓ *A clash between your personality and those of your colleagues (but especially your boss).* It's an old adage that people don't quit organizations, they quit bosses. Even if your organization has a fantastic reputation, a great pension scheme, and great offices, even if you get a buzz from your day-to-day tasks and activities, a bad boss can make your working life a misery. Many employees feel that their bosses are evil, sadistic, ignorant fiends; many bosses feel that their employees are stupid, unmotivated, bungling hooligans. The reality is often somewhere in between. Either manage and tame your boss (Q91, Q92), or quit.

✓ *A disparity between your values and those of your organization.* No matter how much you like the work you do and the people around you, you aren't going to thrive if your organization asks you to behave in a way that does not sit with your values. Suppose you enjoy dealing with customers and have a great boss, but your organization encourages telling lies to customers to push up profits. Imagine if you like brainstorming ideas and enjoy working with your colleagues, but you don't like the fact that your organization measures you on individual rather than team results. Clashes between your values and those of your organization will only lead to grief.

Such reasons may appear trite on paper. Unfortunately, most people choose simply to grumble about their jobs, their immediate teams, or their organizations. There's a big difference between recognizing a problem and doing something about it. Which are you going to do?

1 Should I fake enthusiasm at work?

In a perfect world, you shouldn't have to – you would find yourself in a job that you can feel genuinely enthusiastic about. But in the meantime, I would recommend that you fake enthusiasm for your work.

People are paid to pretend all the time. Tired flight attendants put on smiles even for rude and demanding passengers. Call centre staff feign calm in the face of yet more customer complaints. Shop assistants in department stores, waitstaff in restaurants, hairdressers, public relations consultants, receptionists – people are paid to fake enthusiasm at work.

Psychologists even have a name for the effort required to produce emotions you don't feel and suppress ones you do feel: "emotional labor." And if customer-facing staff are taught to feign enthusiasm with people outwardly, so should you. Treat your bosses and colleagues as you would do customers – smile, be happy, be glad.

I once coached a lawyer who had spotted the importance of emotional labor with colleagues. When she gained her legal qualifications, she got a job with a top law firm. Despite being highly qualified and decidedly well-paid, she complained that all she and the other trainees seemed to be doing was photocopying. But, eventually, when the senior lawyers saw fit to hand bits of more interesting work to the trainees, who do you think they asked first? The ones who had been reluctant to do the photocopying or the ones who had appeared only too pleased to photocopy?

Think of it another way. Focus not on faking enthusiasm, but of downplaying negative emotions. If you can put on a brave face when given tedious, menial, or downright unpleasant tasks you make your boss feel a little less guilty. No one is asking you to pretend you are overjoyed at the prospect, but at least do the tasks with good grace. Think of it simply as an extension of the politeness you exhibit when a loved one cooks you a meal that is inedible or buys you a present that you don't like. Even if both of you know that you're faking it, allowing your boss to feel a little less badly is effectively a good turn banked in your favor.

Faking enthusiasm (or, more correctly, downplaying how you really feel) will help you to get ahead. If you can't get out of a job, you may as well get ahead.

> Treat your bosses and colleagues as you would do customers – smile, be happy, be glad.

2 Do I need a career plan?

A personal development plan is a tool used by organizations to encourage you to develop yourself in ways that help organizations to achieve *their* goals, not yours. Which might have been fine 20 years ago when your success would have been intertwined with the fortunes of your employer. But as downsizing, restructuring, outsourcing, and other ways to cull the workforce become more and more common, the days of the job for life are gone.

The good news is that old-style job security has been squeezed out by New Economy opportunity. In the old days, you had to bide your time, waiting until you had enough years of experience, before you could inch up the career ladder. Nowadays, you find new opportunities on the strength of what you can do, not how long you have been around. Say goodbye to spoon-feeding by your organization and say hello to self-reliance.

Unfortunately, most people give their cars a service more frequently than they service their careers. Most people are too "busy" doing their day-to-day jobs to make any plans. But that's precisely why most people never amount to much.

If this book can impress upon you only one point, it is to take control and assume responsibility for your career. So the answer to the question is of course: yes, you need a career plan. Decide what you want from your career and take steps to achieve it. *Hoping* that good things will happen is not a career strategy.

Imagine that you are the Chairman and CEO, Human Resources and Marketing Director of your own career. It is up to you to set a vision for where you want to be in the future and to carve out a strategy for getting there. You are responsible for developing yourself and ensuring you have a portfolio of in-demand skills. You are in charge of putting the product that is you in front of the people who matter.

If you wait for what you want to come your way, you will be disappointed. Believe that you should simply focus on doing your job well and you're effectively allowing others to decide your fate. Smart people choose where to drive their careers. They make conscious decisions about how to spend their time and who to spend it with. Be one of the smart people by devising a vision (Q13) and a plan to achieve it.

> # Say goodbye to spoon-feeding by your organization and say hello to self-reliance.

3 How can I stop or avoid drifting in my career?

Many people feel frustrated or bored at work. They grumble but never amount to much because they never do anything about it. But not you. You will take control by identifying a vision for your future. Most high-achievers have visions – they just don't necessarily talk about them.

I admit that the word "vision" sounds rather grand and smacks of management jargon (see also Q77 on jargon). But just because the word has become overused does not mean it is not useful.

A vision is simply a term to describe the *life* you aspire to. To achieve whatever goals you may have in life – and not just your career – you must have an idea, a picture, a dream of what your life would look like if you achieved your goals. It's a cliché to say that life is a journey. But let's run with it for now. If life is a journey, what is your destination? You need to have a good sense of the life you want to be living and the role your work should play within it. Without a sense of where you want to go, how will you know if you are making progress? Working harder and longer won't get you anywhere unless you have an idea of where you want to go.

Of course, no one can predict the future and we may not be able to realize every aspect of our visions precisely, but it gives us something to work towards. Our visions may change over time, but at least they point us in the right general direction.

> # If life is a journey, what is your destination?

A personal vision must represent what you genuinely want to do with your life. It can be easy to inadvertently adopt other people's goals rather than our own. Yes a few people have grand visions to cure cancer or end poverty, but most people have far simpler visions. Perhaps you want to get to the top or set up your own business, or want to work fewer hours to redress the balance between your work and home lives. Family may play a big part in your vision or hardly a role at all. A vision should epitomize your unique goals rather than what others deem socially acceptable.

So allow yourself to dream a little and wonder what your life could look like (Q14). What would you like to be doing with your life?

4 So how can I create my personal vision?

A vision is a broad, inspirational picture of your future – how you would *like* your life to turn out as opposed to how it is *likely* to turn out if you simply continue on your current path.

A practical exercise for uncovering your vision is to project yourself forward into the future. Imagine yourself at a birthday party thrown in your honor say ten or 15 years from now. It's a momentous occasion with friends, family, and colleagues there to celebrate with you. Laughter and joy fill the air, and glasses are raised to toast your life. You've asked a handful of important people in your life to give speeches about you. What would they say about you?

Work through the following steps:

✓ *Find a time and place where you can enjoy a half-hour or so of uninterrupted daydreaming.* Start by choosing key people that represent the most important areas of your life. Are they all to do with family or work, both or neither?

✓ *Write down what you would like these people to say about you at this celebration.* Capture in detail not only a description of your achievements – both in and outside of your work – but also the kind of person you are, the relationships you have built up, why you lived as you did, and a sense of how it all feels to you.

✓ *Allow yourself to imagine and dream.* Avoid merely extrapolating your life into the future based on what your life is like now. Don't worry too much about current constraints either. Envisage how you would *like* your life to turn out. Visions are by their nature supposed to be distant and both somewhat scary yet exhilarating in scope.

✓ *Capture your honest aims and wishes.* This is a private essay and you need never show it to anyone else. Feel free to draft your thoughts, set them aside, and return to them over the course of several days, adding thoughts and ideas as they occur to you.

Take your time with your vision. Perhaps talk to close friends, loved ones, and trusted acquaintances to get ideas too. Find a way to escape your day-to-day concerns to let your mind wander and let yourself wonder. And figure out where you would like to go with your life and work.

> # Envisage how you would *like* your life to turn out.

5 I'm struggling – what aspects of my life should a vision cover?

Coming up with a personal vision can be tough. I'm sorry to say there's no easy way to whip one up. People are complex and to reduce your life down to a trite quiz or a simple checklist would do you no favors.

Most people nowadays are so action-oriented that to sit and think is tough. We are rarely encouraged to take time out, without distraction, to contemplate and reflect on what works well, and think and wonder what could be better. But if you need inspiration, consider at least these five areas of your life:

✓ *Your physical life.* Think about your level of satisfaction with your physical health, fitness, diet, energy levels, and well-being.

✓ *Your psychological life.* Consider your psychological wishes including your moral and spiritual needs. Are you living a life that is in keeping with your values? Are you making time for activities that make you happy as well as successful?

✓ *Your interpersonal life.* Bring to mind the mix of social (e.g.

friends and acquaintances), familial (your parents, any siblings, children, and wider family), and intimate (partner or spouse) relationships you would like for a fulfilling life.

✓ *Your occupational life.* Consider to what extent you need to enjoy your work and get satisfaction from it. Quiz yourself about how your working life could meet more of your life's broader goals.

✓ *Your financial life.* Society pushes us to strive for more money. But consider how much money you actually need to live the kind of lifestyle that would make you happy.

Ensure that your vision at least touches on all five aspects of a balanced life. One-dimensional visions rarely work out. People who strive to achieve only in one area of their life often find that other areas let them down and prevent them from achieving their goals. People who are willing to do whatever it takes to get rich may find their health lets them down or they burn out emotionally. Those who seek only inner peace may find that they can't be very peaceful without earning enough to support their family.

If you aren't going to start looking after every aspect of your life now, when are you going to do it? Don't delude yourself that you will do it *tomorrow* – we all know that tomorrow never comes.

16 What are the pitfalls involved in writing a personal vision?

I know I'm spending a lot of time bleating on about a personal vision, but it really is important, whatever your career goals – whether you want to make CEO, reduce your hours, change career entirely, or something in between.

In shaping your vision, be watchful of the following pitfalls:

✓ *Creating only a career vision.* Notice that your occupational needs are only one part of your overall life's needs (Q15). As such, make sure your vision captures not only your career goals but also your goals outside of work. Unless you are certain you want to throw your entire life's focus and all of your energies into nothing apart from your work, be certain your vision reflects a balanced view of your entire life.

✓ *Succumbing to external pressures.* It's human nature to chase what we think we should or ought to do. But a vision should be your personal blueprint of the future. Just because your peers are chasing bigger salaries should not deter you from pursuing a quieter and simpler life. Just because your friends and family don't think they can do better should not stop you from striving to achieve more. Focus on *your* dreams – not those of the people around you. Ensure that the only pressures to drive you in a particular direction are the ones you are happy to place on yourself.

✓ *Believing a vision has to be complete in every detail.* Even though the visioning exercises (Q14, Q15) encourage you to write down in as much detail as possible how you would like your life to look, it's okay not to have perfect clarity on every aspect of your future life. Your vision can be a bit blurry. The idea of a vision is to create a powerful and vivid sense of the life you would like to live, not to craft something that is so detailed that it becomes prescriptive.

✓ *Limiting yourself to the written word.* If you don't like the idea of writing out your vision, perhaps draw a diagram of your vision, cut out pictures from magazines and paste them into a scrapbook, dictate your thoughts into a voice recorder, or turn your vision into lyrics and set it to music if that floats your boat. Just do it *somehow*.

> # Focus on *your* dreams – not those of the people around you.

17 What's the best way to set effective goals?

Research and experience tells us that defining clear goals dramatically increases our chances of achieving them. Whether you are setting goals to do with a project at work or setting goals to do with your own life and career, be sure to capture exactly what you wish to achieve.

Management experts have been setting SMART goals for decades. But, to bring effective goal setting into the twenty-first century, I recommend that your goals should instead be SPORTY:

✓ *Stretching.* We tend to achieve more when we set ourselves more challenging goals. Aim to set yourself a goal that is neither so easy that you cannot fail to achieve it or so demanding that you are bound to fall short. Aim for a goal that is at least *slightly* daunting.

✓ *Positive.* Successful actions must always be phrased in terms of what you want, e.g. "offer more praise" rather than what you need to avoid, e.g. "don't criticize." It's much more motivating to focus on what we are working towards rather than what we want to move away from.

✓ *Observable.* Make sure that other people could categorically agree whether you had achieved a goal or not. For example, saying that you want to "read more widely about business" is open to debate. How much is "more"? A specific action such as "read the *Harvard Business Review* every month" is observable and allows you to measure whether you are doing it or not.

✓ *Realistic.* Aiming to do 40 hours' worth of studying when you're already working a 60-hour week and trying to look after your family is insane. Look at all of your goals and make sure you are choosing goals that are achievable given your circumstances and any constraints.

✓ *Timed.* The danger of allowing yourself a goal without saying when you will attempt it is that you could legitimately keep putting it off and putting it off. Decide on a realistic time frame to keep you focused on what you must do.

✓ *Yield results.* Finally, check that your activity moves you closer toward your long-term goals (such as those from your vision, see Q13). You can have a specific, positive, observable, realistic and timed goal, but unless it yields results that will have a meaningful impact on your life, it's not really worth doing.

> # Define your goals to give yourself the best chance of achieving them.

8 How can I figure out whether to accept a new job offer?

Congratulate yourself if you have received a job offer. But before you sign on the dotted line, be very sure that this really is the right job for you. More than one professional has been caught up in the excitement of a job offer and been swayed by the promises of a prospective employer, forgetting that most employers will not willingly own up to the downsides of the job.

Remember that accepting a job offer effectively ties you in to an employer for at least a year. Future employers may be wary of hiring you if you skip out on an employer too quickly. So don't let yourself get trapped into making the wrong career move.

Conduct your own career due diligence by visiting the organization as many times as you need. Of course meet with your potential boss but, more importantly, get to know your prospective peers. While future bosses tend to be quite guarded and may choose their words carefully, the rest of the team may be more willing to expose the possibly seedy side of the organization. Take them for group drinks or one-to-one lunches and get them talking. Assure them that what they say will never get back to their boss and quiz them on their frustrations about the job, their gripes about the organization, and the low-down on what the boss is really like to work for.

People tend to become unhappy in their work for one of three key reasons (see Q10 for elaboration on those reasons). Be sure of the match between:

1. *Your strengths and the daily demands of the job.* Are you happy that you will be spending your time on tasks you enjoy?

2. *Your personality and that of your boss and colleagues.* Do you think you be able to put up – or even have fun – with your colleagues?

3. *Your values and those of the organization.* Are you sure the organization's attitude to risk, its reward and promotion philosophy, its treatment of employees during times of change, and so on are in keeping with your own?

9 Should I bother hiring a professional coach?

I work as a business and life coach. So believe me when I say that hiring a coach should not be your first resort. Yes, coaches can be a powerful resource in bringing about change in your career and life. But before approaching a professional coach, I would strongly urge you to work through the following steps:

1. *Try to change on your own.* This book contains all of the resources you need to find your own solution without having to pay for the services of a coach. Consider creating an inspiring vision of what you want to achieve (Q13). Turn your vision into a series of SPORTY goals against which you can measure your progress (Q17). And turn your concrete goals into an action plan that you can implement on a daily basis (Q44).

2. *Draw upon the resources of trusted acquaintances.* Get feedback and ideas from people whose opinions you trust (Q42). And, if you feel that they genuinely have your best interests at heart, share your goals with them and ask if they will support you. They may be able to offer you practical assistance, training,

and advice, or perhaps help to motivate you and keep you on track.

3. *Seek the advice of a mentor.* People further up the organization may be willing to act as mentors in guiding your career. Having a mentor is possibly the best-kept secret of career success. Think about people both within and outside of your organization who might be willing to mentor you (Q88). Many senior managers have coaches solely because they are at the top of the career ladder and can't easily find people even more experienced than themselves to mentor them.

I'm not saying that those three steps are easy. But many people do set out to change their careers and succeed on their own. Only once you have at least tried to work through those three steps should you think about paying a coach to guide you.

Should I get involved with office politics?

Office politics gets a bad rep. Ask people what they think it means and they are quick to mention backstabbing, scheming, maneuvering, rumor-mongering, plotting, cheating, lying, and being two-faced.

Yes, all of those tactics are employed in the workplace, but that does not mean that all office politics is automatically bad. Office politics is not witchcraft – it's a tool just as a knife is a tool. A knife is neither inherently good nor bad – it can be used by a surgeon to cut away cancerous tissue or wielded by an attacker mugging someone on the street. Office politics is merely the skill of understanding and using the structure, relationships, and personalities within an organization to achieve results. Put simply, politics is achieving results through relationships – getting stuff done through people. Whether you choose to pursue mutually beneficial goals or achieve selfish goals that undermine others is up to you. Be the life-loving surgeon or the life-threatening mugger at work, the choice is yours.

Perhaps a better term than "office politics" is "lobbying" – using personal relationships, power, authority, your profile within the organization (Q75), and an understanding of what makes different people tick to affect outcomes.

> # Put simply, politics is achieving results through relationships.

People do not always go through formal channels to get what they want. If working through a formal channel may be too bureaucratic or time-consuming or simply not deliver the right outcome, people will look to use informal channels such as personal relationships.

Given the intense competition for scarce resources and opportunities within most organizations, politicking is unavoidable. Whether you are gathering support from senior colleagues for a project to benefit the organization, or chasing a promotion or an exciting assignment for yourself, you will find that ignoring office politics will make life that much more difficult for you.

21 What are the essential rules of office politics?

Even if you don't intend to get proactively involved in politics at work, at least make sure you do not cause unintentional offence or get caught up in the machinations of your colleagues. Here are five basic principles to help you navigate the minefield of politics without losing a limb:

1. *Avoid choosing sides.* If you work in a highly political environment, aim to be the Switzerland of the organizational world. Deciding that you are "for" one person or team necessarily means you are "against" others. If at all possible, do what is best for the organization rather than allowing yourself to be dragged into power struggles and disagreements.

2. *Maintain a "no surprises" policy.* Ensure you communicate both the good news and bad to your boss and others who need to be informed. People would much rather know what has gone wrong than look stupid later on.

3. *Make senior people feel good.* It's more important to make your

bosses and other important people feel good about their relationships with you than to prove to them that you are right. In debates and discussions, learn to concede and back down gracefully well before you are in danger of causing offence.

4. *Look beneath the surface.* The reasons people give for the ways they behave do not always represent the whole story. Understand that people have both public and personal agendas. Sure, the people in another team may understand that reducing the size of their budget is the right thing to do for the organization, but what they may not privately be so happy about is that they lose status too. When trying to move people forward on an issue, make sure to look at not only the publicly stated reasons they give but also the emotional reasons they may be reluctant to share.

5. *Always be seen to be committed to organizational goals.* People hate feeling manipulated and detest individuals who they see as self-serving. The easiest way not to be seen as self-interested is to make sure your actions genuinely advance organizational goals. If you have dark personal aims of your own, at least have the good sense to be discreet about them. And remember that it's far easier to erode trust than to win it back.

> # Understand that people have both public and personal agendas.

22 How can I develop my political savvy?

Q21 covered some of the basic rules that will keep you out of political crossfires. But if you want to engage more proactively with politics in advancing either organizational or personal goals, here are some further pointers to help you get your way:

✓ *Consider the needs of the wider team.* Sometimes an issue can be decided by a small number of people but affect many others. Make a list of all the people who may be affected by an issue and consult them too.

✓ *Seek involvement as early as possible.* People are much more likely to agree with your point of view if they feel emotionally invested in it. If you present to colleagues a plan of action you have already decided on, they have little to lose by saying no to it. However, if you first plant the seed of an idea and seek their help in formulating the plan of action, they are more likely to say yes to it.

✓ *Seek dialogue through both formal and informal channels.* Sometimes the best way to understand other people's personal agendas is simply to ask. What people are willing to say in a meeting in front of their bosses or peers may be different to what they disclose in a private, one-to-one, "off-the-record" conversation.

✓ *Learn to recognize both spoken and unspoken signs of resistance.* People's non-verbal cues can often be a bigger giveaway as to how they feel than what they say. Read people's body language and respond accordingly.

✓ *Identify which battles are worth fighting.* Keep the bigger picture and your long-term goals in mind. When it comes to any particular issue, always weigh up the short-term benefits of winning an argument versus any possible longer-term consequences. As the saying goes, be careful not to win a battle but lose the war.

✓ *Aim to pull rather than push people toward goals.* Even if you have the authority to do so, strive to "pull" people towards goal by setting an example, appealing to their better natures, or exciting them about possibilities. Avoid "push" tactics such as relying on the strength of a purely logical argument, making demands or even threats (see Q69).

The best way to understand other people's personal agendas is simply to ask.

---

23 How can I get colleagues to agree to my plans?

When you feel that a project is too important to risk having it shot down by others, make sure you invest time and energy in involving the right people at the right time:

✓ *Get a second opinion.* Before presenting any important idea at a meeting, talk it through with a colleague whose opinion you value (such as a mentor, see Q87). Ask your colleague to critique your idea and expose its weaknesses so you can strengthen your argument for wider consumption.

✓ *Be clear about your agenda.* Question your own motives and ensure that others will have no reasons to doubt why you may be supporting a project. Work out a way to explain how the project will be good for the overall organization rather than just yourself or your own team.

✓ *Invite skeptics as well as supporters to come on board.* When setting up a project team or a task force, consider who should be invited. There's a real risk in involving only supporters of the project as the skeptics will probably stir up trouble elsewhere. Sure, involving the troublemakers may slow discussions down considerably, but at least you can hear their objections and deal with any problems directly. You know what they say about keeping your enemies close.

✓ *Talk to key stakeholders individually.* List everyone who will be affected by your project. If there are key individuals amongst your peers or higher management who could derail your plans, make sure you give them the chance to speak by seeking their views in one-to-one discussions.

When it comes to seeking support for a project or initiative, bear in mind the trade-off between its pace and likelihood of success. The quicker you try to move forward, the more likely people are to resist. If you want to succeed, expect to spend a lot of time consulting people, listening to their concerns, and looking for ways to keep everybody happy.

24 How can I escape the ranks of middle management?

Moving from the bottleneck of middle management into senior management means a move away from doing work to building capability, from focusing on what needs doing today to what might need doing tomorrow. Of course there's a careful juggling act to be done, but speed your continuing progress within the organization by learning to:

✓ *Build the skills of other people.* Junior managers delegate work. However, delegation is not a long-term strategy for success because the people who work for you learn only to accept instruction. Smart managers coach the members of their teams; they focus on building the skills and confidence of their teams to create successors. Try telling your team only what you want them to do and allow them to work out how best to do it; encourage them to come up with their own ways of tackling issues and opportunities, allow for them to make mistakes but learn and grow too. While coaching takes time in the short-term, successful managers realize that doing so improves the ability of the team to do more in the long-term (see also Q60 on giving constructive criticism). And building a reputation as someone who develops successors will boost your profile no end.

✓ *Spend more time looking outwards.* Of course you're networking within your organization right? But move your focus now to networking externally with customers, competitors, and suppliers within your industry as well as outside of your sector (see Q51). Senior managers don't reach the tops of organizations by merely repeating what they've been doing so far. So look for new ideas and trends from elsewhere. Interact with others and look, listen, and absorb. You never know where your next brilliant inspiration may come from. See what your organization could learn about marketing from a pharmaceuticals business, finance from a carmaker, or human resources from a management consultancy.

✓ *Think "big picture."* Move your focus gradually away from implementing what needs doing to considering possibilities. While you still need to focus on your current business objectives, look to take a much broader and longer-term view in considering the widest possible range of alternatives, threats and opportunities that could affect your organization. In the same way that you may perhaps have a personal vision (Q13) of where you want to be in ten or 15 years' time, start to ask more questions about where your organization needs to be in a similar time frame.

25 Should I write goals down?

Yes, yes, emphatically yes. Whatever your goals, I urge you to write them down. Your goal may be to do with completing a project successfully. Maybe you want to learn certain skills or acquire particular experiences to further your career. Perhaps you have a very specific goal to quit a bad habit or a very broad goal to do with your work and also your life outside of it (see Q15). Whether you wish to set small daily goals or grand annual ones, write them down.

If you want to achieve your goals, the nature of your goals matter less than the fact that you write them down. I won't bore you with too much science in this book, but this bit is important so bear with me. Back in the 1950s, researchers questioned graduates from Harvard University as to how many of them had goals. As you would expect, almost all of them had goals. But when they asked them how many of them wrote those goals down, only 3 percent of them said they did. To cut a long story short, a follow-up survey 30 years later discovered that the 3 percent who had put pen to paper had amassed as much wealth as the other 97 percent put together.

Wow. Of course money can't necessarily buy happiness, but still – wow.

Capturing goals in print crystallizes your intentions. It cements your goals, kicks you into action, and makes you 20 times more likely to do it. I write goals down. Will you?

26 How can I manage my time better and become more productive?

Some people rush around from meeting to meeting, drawing up plans, talking about how busy and stressed they are and how much they have to do, but they never seem to achieve much. However, there's a big difference between being busy and effective, between activity and productivity.

Don't be fooled into thinking you could ever squeeze more tasks into your day. There are only 24 hours in a day and, assuming you need to sleep and eat occasionally, you only have a finite amount of time to tackle the tasks you may want to do. Sure, there are particular time management tools that help you to organize your tasks more effectively (Q30), but they only tinker at the edges of what you need to do to become truly productive.

Rather than trying to achieve *more* in the same amount of time, change your way of thinking to achieving *more of what is important to you.* By definition, this means spending less time on distractions and tasks that are unimportant.

Learning to separate tasks that are *important* as opposed to *urgent* (Q27) allows people to prioritize how to spend their time and become more productive. But this assumes that you have a clear picture in your mind as to what is important to you. Having a vision (Q13) plus some life and career goals (Q17) is an essential foundation for learning to become more productive. Without a vision, you risk spending all your time helping your organization to achieve its goals, without ever achieving your own.

> # There's a big difference between being busy and effective, between activity and productivity.

Consider the difference between urgency and importance. Say a colleague phones you to pass on a piece of gossip. The phone call is urgent because it's difficult to ignore a ringing telephone, but is it important to you? Does spending time on the conversation help to further your career and your life goals? Possibly not.

On the other hand, taking the time to update your CV and speak to people within your network about new job opportunities may not be urgent. It can wait for a day or two, and then a day or two after that as well, and the days become weeks and months. But of course it's important if you have particular career goals.

Urgent needs scream for our attention and we often give in to tackling them. Important needs sit quietly in the background, but are the ones that can truly take us closer to our goals.

27 Why should I focus on *important* rather than *urgent* tasks?

Focus on *important* tasks and you will succeed in advancing your career and life goals. Focus on merely *urgent* tasks and you will get tired and stressed.

		Low Urgency	High Urgency
Importance	High	**2:** Important tasks	**1:** Important and urgent tasks
	Low	**4:** Tasks that are neither important nor urgent	**3:** Urgent (but not important) tasks

Urgency

Consider the two-by-two grid above and the consequences of spending your time in each of the four quadrants:

✓ 1. *Important and urgent tasks.* There will be work and life demands that require immediate attention such as a crisis in the office or at home, a major problem, perhaps a time-critical opportunity, or simply project work or meetings that are now due. Most people are able to identify these and respond to these as necessary. However, the truth is that we rarely face tasks that are both urgent and important.

✓ 2. *Important tasks.* Into this box go all of the tasks and activities that will help you to meet the long-term goals contained within your vision. If, for example, you wish to get a promotion, you may need to cultivate particular relationships within your organization, chase project opportunities, or pursue training and development activities. If you wish to set up your own business, perhaps you need to spend time networking externally. If your vision encompasses your physical health, you may need to plan for exercise or eating healthily. Your psychological health may demand certain leisure activities. Your interpersonal life may require an investment in spending time with friends. Putting off any of these activities may have few immediate consequences on your life – you're not going to die or get fired immediately. But without actively investing in box 2 activities, you will not achieve your life's ambitions.

✓ 3. *Urgent (but not important) tasks.* Such tasks may be important to other people, but ask yourself whether they are important to *you*. A colleague may invite you to a meeting, but what would happen if you declined to attend at all? A friend may send an email asking about your plans for the weekend, but what would happen if you were to put off responding until the end of the week? Many emails, phone calls, meetings and interruptions can either be delegated or avoided entirely (see Q73 on saying "no").

✓ *4. Tasks that are neither important nor urgent.* No one is suggesting that you cease to participate in office conversations and an occasional bit of idle internet surfing. But make an effort to cut down on box 4 activities and you may find yourself freeing up a fair amount of time to invest in more important activities.

28 So what does effective time management look like in practice?

Time management becomes a lot easier when you know what is important in your life and can plan how to use your time. Here's a step-by-step guide to doing it:

1. At the end of each day, write a list of all the tasks you need to do for the next day. Wait until the next morning when you arrive at work before writing your list and you may possibly get sucked immediately into urgent tasks.

2. Allocate your different tasks to the four boxes indicated in the importance/urgency grid (Q27).

3. Group related activities together. Rather than making a phone call then writing a report and returning to yet another phone call, plan to make all of your phone calls at once, deal with all emails at once, and so on.

4. Plan a way of setting aside blocks of time during your day to focus only on your important tasks, such as by setting up an interruption-free zone (Q29).

5. Begin your day with the first task in box 1. When you have completed it, continue with the rest of your tasks in box 1 until you have completed them all.

6. Only when you have completed your box 1 tasks should you move on to the tasks in box 2. Continue to move through your box 2 activities until you have completed them too.

7. Focus on only one task at a time and work on it ruthlessly to the exclusion of everything else until it has been completed. To retain your focus and remain effective, avoid dipping in and out of different tasks.

8. At the end of the day, review the results you achieved and reflect (Q45) on lessons for creating a plan for the next day.

Planning doesn't mean scheduling a list of tasks that you will do regardless of what happens at work – if something important *and* urgent comes up, of course you reprioritise. However, it does mean making a conscious effort to control your day rather than letting the priorities and demands of other people dictate what you end up achieving. And yes, it takes time to plan – perhaps five or ten minutes every evening – but it's an investment of time that will pay dividends over the course of the next day.

29 How can I create an interruption-free zone at work?

To allow yourself to focus on whatever important tasks you may have on any given day, try these pointers for creating an interruption-free environment at work:

✓ Check your email only at scheduled points in the day, for example once in the morning, once at lunchtime, and a final time at the end of the day. Turn off any automatic notifications and switch off the BlackBerry too. You, not your computer, should determine when to deal with your emails. Dealing with all of your emails at once is a more productive strategy than dealing with them individually as they arrive.

✓ Identify when you are most productive at work. Are you a morning or afternoon person? Then set up a time slot during which you can aim to avoid external interruptions. Perhaps arrive an hour earlier if you are a morning person or stay later than your colleagues if you prefer evenings. During this time, divert your mobile and desk phones to voicemail for several hours.

✓ Stop yourself every time any new task interrupts what you are doing. Ask yourself whether it is important and urgent enough to warrant immediate action or can wait.

✓ Train your colleagues to leave you in peace during your most productive hours. Each time a colleague interrupts you, tell them that you're busy and ask if their request can wait until after a certain time of day. Even better if you can close your door or put a sign on your desk that says, "Busy right now, can it wait until after 11am?" Persist in reminding your colleagues of your no-interruption slot until they learn not to bother you unless they absolutely must from 9am till 11am, 2pm till 3.30pm, or whatever slot(s) you can manage every day.

In practice, it is impossible to enforce interruption-free periods all of the time and plan your day down to the last detail. No matter how proactive you are in planning your day, new important and urgent demands will come your way. However, that does not mean that you should give up. Review at the end of the day what worked well and carry the lessons forward to the next. So, what are you going to do today?

> # Train your colleagues to leave you in peace during your most productive hours.

30 How can I tame the paperwork monster?

Internal memos, customer reports, management information print-offs, technical papers, articles we keep meaning to read, and assorted documents have a habit of building up on our desks without us noticing. Your email inbox and hard drive are probably fighting a second front against the virtual paperwork monster too.

To reduce the amount of time you spend dealing with paperwork of either the physical or electronic kind, remember only one key principle: *Touch simple items only once.* If a memo or email comes your way and you read it, add it to a list of tasks to be completed later, come back to it later, re-read it, then action it, you effectively triple the amount of work you are doing. Instead, set aside a time each day or week (Q29) to deal with your administration and use the RAFT acronym. Touch each item only once and choose to refer, act, file or trash it:

✓ *Refer.* If an item is the responsibility of another person or needs to be seen by someone else, forward it on immediately.

✓ *Act.* If an item is your responsibility, act on it immediately. As a rule of thumb, if it can be handled within five minutes, deal with it straightaway. Only if it requires more serious attention should you add it to your list of tasks for either that day or the next (see Q28 on making effective lists).

✓ *File.* If an item does not require action but must be saved for future reference purposes, file it. Work out simple systems for both physical and electronic documents that will allow you to retrieve items at a later date. The key to effective filing is to ask yourself where you would be most likely to look for it in the future.

✓ *Trash.* You will find that the vast majority of items that come to you can be discarded straightaway. While you may agonize about needing an item in the future, be ruthless with it. Ask yourself whether you really need it or are simply afraid to let it go. Chances are you will never need it and if you do, you will probably be able to retrieve a copy of the original from whoever sent it to you in the first place.

> # The vast majority of items that come to you can be discarded straightaway.

31 How much socializing do I have to do with my work "buddies"?

In an ideal world, socializing would be an optional activity dependent purely on how much you enjoy spending time with colleagues. In reality, little that is connected with work is without consequence. Socializing insufficiently or in the wrong way could have implications for your career.

The importance and type of socializing that goes on within an organization is usually bound up with its culture. Like many other aspects of culture (Q6), the amount and form of socializing you need to do will never be written down. I also doubt that anyone would ever tell you that you aren't spending enough time with your colleagues. But that doesn't mean that it doesn't go unnoticed.

I used to work for an American firm that thought it so important for colleagues to get on with each other that the firm paid for groups of us to go away on annual "bonding" weekends together. In your organization, you may find that drinks every Friday evening, attendance at colleagues' leaving lunches, or perhaps elegant dinner parties are a vital part of maintaining your standing in the office. I know of an investment bank that not only turned a blind eye but practically encouraged its analysts to visit a strip joint together.

If half of the office is heading to the bar, salsa class, or whatever, while you're heading to the gym, a parent–teacher evening, or home, you may end up losing out. Your colleagues are bonding, building bridges, getting to know each other personally. And knowing someone personally is only a short step away from promoting them or entrusting them with that glamorous project in the overseas office. Success at work often comes down to relationships at work (Q1), so make sure you soak up the atmosphere and show that you fit in with the rest of the team.

> # Knowing someone personally is only a short step away from promoting them.

32 What's the best way to express complaints at work?

No one likes a moaner. Every office has a couple of them – the grumpy workers who shuffle from office to office spreading their contagion of whining, complaints, and even paranoia. Make sure you're not one of them.

By all means raise issues with colleagues in a professional manner if there are problems that stop you from doing your job. If your computer crashes considerably more than those of your colleagues, that's a genuine problem; having a computer that is old and equally as out-of-date as those of your colleagues is not. Having the marketing department consistently put your requests to the bottom of the heap may be cause for concern, but having insufficient marketing budget for yourself or anyone else to have their requests dealt with satisfactorily is a problem that is out of your hands. You get the idea.

You will always find workers who vent their frustrations and feel that it brings them sympathy. But expressing sympathy is not the same as showing approval. Demonstrating compassion is not the same as endorsing their skills and recommending them for more exciting opportunities.

No matter how much others moan about their work, resist doing the same. Bosses and colleagues value enthusiasm (see also Q11). They are naturally drawn to people who are happy and positive. If you talk about how much work you have on, how tough a project is, how unfair a decision was, the people around you might secretly wish you'd shut up. Trust me, they're not going to pop by your desk for a chat again. Complaining marks you out as a troublemaker – do troublemakers get promoted? Even when colleagues wander by and ask how you are, bear in mind that they probably don't want to know. It's simply a greeting and the appropriate response is to tell them how well you are.

The person who points out that a project is not going to work is never popular either. If you can see that an idea is not going to work, do nothing, say nothing, stall for time. The project will eventually die when its instigator realizes that it is a lost cause. But be the one to point it out first and you may well cause your relationship with the project's backer to fray. Your objections may be correct, but remember that people frequently do shoot the messenger.

> Complaining marks you out as a troublemaker – do troublemakers get promoted?

33 How much does appearance really matter at work?

What you wear and how you look *should* matter less than your ability to do the job. But appearance does matter.

Your colleagues' appearances – from clothes to style of hair and choice of accessories – are often the surface manifestation of an organization's culture (see also Q4). Wearing the same clothes as the people around you shows that you "fit," that you blend in and deserve to be there, that you're one of the team.

Of course you may want to prove that you are an individual and succeed on your own merits. But why make life difficult for yourself? Competition is tough enough so prove your point after you've made it to the top.

But make sure you show that you're part of the *right* team. Most organizations are divided along lines that may have little to do with the official hierarchy. Are you a "creative" or a "suit"? Client-facing or support staff? An aspiring manager or a past-it manager?

Whether your colleagues spend their cash on thrift store bargains or designer couture, make sure you do the same. If your self-important colleagues wear double cuff shirts, you do too; if your no-nonsense colleagues like a dash of polyester in their clothes, that's the way you go too. A practical laptop bag may say "sensible" in one organization but "dull" in another; conversely, an elegant calfskin attaché case may say "essential" in one but "trying too hard" in another. You get the picture.

On the other hand, don't obsess about what you wear. Some personal branding (Q94) gurus recommend wearing something distinctive so that people can associate you with, say, wearing red ties or purple eye shadow. But do you really want to be remembered solely for what you look like? Of course not.

Dressing and looking the same as your colleagues is about making sure you do not stand out for the wrong reasons; even spending a fortune to emulate your bosses won't get you promoted if you're rubbish at the job.

34 Should I focus on my strengths or work on my weaknesses?

No one, however talented, is perfectly well-rounded. We all have unique strengths as well as weaknesses – weaknesses of which we are probably all too well aware. How often have colleagues or bosses criticized you or given you "feedback" on the same shortcomings? How many times have you sat in performance appraisals and been reminded yet again of the same old "development needs"? Organizations, our bosses, and colleagues, are obsessed with helping employees understand their weaknesses. They persist in believing that weaknesses can be fixed.

Interestingly enough, there is a growing body of research that says that you simply shouldn't bother trying to work on your weaknesses. The late Don Clifton of the Gallup Organization in the United States argued that there is simply no evidence to suggest that everyone can become good at anything, even given plenty of training and development.

Our own experience tells us that too. There are some tasks that make us feel as if time is dragging by – we feel we have to force

> # Discover and develop what is *right* about you; don't sweat about the rest.

ourselves to persist at them and feel relieved when we finally accomplish them. Often, we may take twice as long to do a task as some of our colleagues do, and possibly not even do it half as well. For example, I don't like much the process of financial forecasting. Poring over financial forecasts feels like much harder work for me than meeting with clients, coaching people, or speaking in public. Spending hundreds of hours learning more about financial forecasting would bore me and little of it would lodge in my brain. So why bother?

If you want to be both happy and successful, look for ways to use more of your strengths in your work (see Q37 to discover yours). Talk to your boss about changing the duties of your role, move into a different team, or change jobs entirely. The more you enjoy what you do, the more likely you will be to excel. It sounds so obvious when you see it written down – but then why do so few people concentrate on their strengths rather than dwell on their weaknesses?

Our weaknesses are weak for a reason – perhaps something from our childhoods means that we may never enjoy or get much better at particular skills. So don't focus on your weaknesses. Discover and develop what is *right* about you; don't sweat about the rest.

35 How can I manage my weaknesses?

Just because fulfillment and success are more likely to come from focusing on your strengths (Q34) does not mean that you can necessarily ignore all of your weaknesses.

If your job requires a certain level of basic competence in a skill, consider some of these tactics for managing your weaknesses:

✓ *Develop a system to cope with it.* If you aren't naturally the most organized person in the world, buy a wall planner, chart, filing system, or handheld organizer that forces you to organize yourself better. If you find it difficult to get your points across during meetings, write yourself a checklist of questions to help you prepare your thoughts before every meeting. If you find it difficult to see what is positive about another person's arguments, write in large letters across the top of your notepad a reminder to make at least two encouraging comments before uttering a negative. Look for a way to mimic what others do naturally. You will never be as good at a skill by covering up a lack of talent as someone who has the talent naturally, but you may be able to do it well enough to get by.

✓ *Find a partner.* If you are good with people but struggle with numbers, find someone within your organization who is great with them and trade favors. Help your more numerate colleague by using one of the strengths he or she lacks in return. If you enjoy coming up with new ideas but aren't very good at implementing them, work with a colleague who enjoys execution rather than conception.

✓ *Communicate your weakness to others and move on.* Tell people how challenging you find a particular skill and encourage others to help you work around it. If you find it difficult to empathize with other people's problems, tell your colleagues that you may not always be able to tell what they are feeling and that they need to speak up if they aren't happy. If you know that you are great at planning and organizing in advance but not so good in a crisis, say so and let your colleagues deal with emergencies. Confessing your weaknesses may even win you respect for not trying to pretend to be perfect and a person that you are not.

However, for those occasions in which you can't manage a weakness and need to develop at least a basic level of competence in a skill, see Q44 on assembling self-improvement plans.

36 Why do I need to understand my signature strengths?

Most of us would be a lot more fulfilled and successful if we could only play to our strengths. If you can find a way to get paid to do what you love, you're onto a winner.

Wanting to be successful won't make you successful, but enjoying what you do might just do it. Consider for a moment multi-millionaire business people who have "made it." They often have more money than they could ever need, yet continue to work because they enjoy what they do. Their enjoyment of their work allowed them to become successful – not the other way around.

Unfortunately, most of us find it easier to recall our weaknesses because they cause us problems and difficulties; we typically find it more difficult to identify our true strengths because we find those skills easy and may discount them or not even be aware of them.

In trying to identify your strengths, be sure not to confuse mere skills with strengths. Consider the difference between a skill and an interest:

✓ *Skill.* A skill is what you are good at, your ability to accomplish certain tasks. Perhaps your skills are at a sufficient level for you to get paid for using them. But simply being good at what you do does not mean that you necessarily enjoy it. Just because you are able to calculate budgets does not mean that you should make it your calling in life.

✓ *Interest.* An interest is what you enjoy doing, the stuff that makes a task fun or satisfying. Your interests may lie in topics that fascinate you and compel you to learn more about them. You have an innate curiosity and find it easy to lose track of time when pursuing your interests.

Consequently, your strengths can be defined as the areas in which your skills and interests coincide (see Q37 to identify yours). When you exercise skills in which you also have interest, you will feel engaged, motivated, and passionate – and you may become successful too.

> # If you can find a way to get paid to do what you love, you're on to a winner.

37 What are my signature strengths?

Utilizing your strengths will help you be successful as well as satisfied. The following story-telling exercise takes time, but will help you to identify your strengths:

1. *Create a retrospective chronological log of your life to date.* Take a notepad and write the current year "20__" at the top of the first page. On the next page, write the dates of the previous two years. Then turn to the next page and write the previous two years to that. For example, if you are reading this in the year 2017, write "2017" on the first page, then "2015 to 2016" on the second page, "2013 to 2014" on the third, and so on. Keep writing the years until you have reached the years of your childhood.

2. *List your main life activities within each time period.* For each two-year period write down, for example, the positions you held at work, the schools you attended, along with non-work activities such as moving house, getting married, or learning a musical instrument.

3. *List your accomplishments within each time period.* Write down every accomplishment during each time period. Keep your

definition of your accomplishments deliberately broad, to encompass anything you achieved no matter how big or small. It could be anything that you were responsible for or were proud of having done, both in your work and outside of it.

4. *Keep listing more accomplishments.* Aim to have roughly twice as many accomplishments as your age. Yes, I know that may seem a lot, but you must list all of your accomplishments, no matter how unrelated to work or trivial they might at first seem.

Once you have listed all of your accomplishments, look at your list and decide which ones you enjoyed achieving. Take each of those accomplishments in turn and write a couple of paragraphs describing what you did to attain your accomplishment. Write it out in the first person as if you were relating the story to a friend or speak your thoughts into a voice recorder. It will take you a while, but it's worth the effort.

Finally, look at your stories and look particularly at the verbs you used in each. By looking at the actions you took, you can begin to piece together a picture of your strengths – your favored skills and personal qualities. Look for themes that span across different accomplishments. Consider your strengths, which could be anything from communicating through writing or creating with your hands to organizing projects, identifying problems, or entertaining others.

38 How else can I discover my signature strengths?

Given the importance of identifying your signature strengths so that you can shape the right career for yourself, here are two alternative or perhaps complementary exercises for discovering them:

✓ *Ask other people why they value you.* We often find it difficult to see ourselves with any objectivity. Make a list of a dozen people who know you well. Choose people both from your work life and outside of it as you may have strengths that you have never had the opportunity to display in your personal life (or vice versa). Tell each person that you are engaged in some personal development work and ask them: "What is it that you most value about me?" When you talk to people about what they value about you, they may initially come up with lots of adjectives such as the fact that you are "charming" or "helpful," "persistent" or "inquisitive." However, encourage them to tell you examples of when you demonstrated those traits and listen to the verbs they use to describe what you did. Those stories (and particularly the verbs) may hold within them clues as to your strengths.

✓ *Use the table below to* prompt *yourself about possible strengths.* Avoid simply choosing words from the following list that you think represent your strengths. Working out how you have used those skills to attain enjoyable accomplishments (Q36) is a more reliable way to identify your strengths.

Researching	Analyzing	Initiating
Budgeting	Planning	Leading others
Repairing	Influencing	Speaking (in public)
Implementation	Administration	Mentoring
Coaching	Being creative	Managing projects
Debating	Writing	Motivating
Problem solving	Selling	Competing
Communicating	Innovating	Decision making
Negotiating	Working in a team	Facilitating
Operating	Installing	Remaining positive
Compiling	Evaluating	Constructing
Interpreting	Entertaining	Serving
Supervising	Empathizing	Purchasing
Learning	Calculating	Helping
Persisting	Imagining	Editing
Conceptualizing	Reviewing	Adapting
Challenging	Supporting	Strategizing
Promoting	Including (others)	Listening

Of course, no list can ever be totally comprehensive, so add your own words to it as well. Your strengths are unique to you and no one else. But what are they?

39 How can I progress quickly from the bottom rung of the career ladder?

When you start out in your career, bear in mind that you begin as a nobody. However, a simple set of rules can help you to stand out from your peers. While the following advice may at first appear obvious, I would say from experience that the difficulty is not in understanding the rules, but in applying them unswervingly:

✓ *Beware any feelings of entitlement.* Clever entry-level employees with good educational backgrounds sometimes feel they should be entitled to interesting work. Wrong. When you begin your career, you have no rights, no privileges. Even if you have been recruited as a high-flyer, you begin with less standing than the post room workers and receptionists.

✓ *Be enthusiastic and positive.* If there is a trivial, menial, or even occasionally demeaning job, it will probably fall to you. But that's the way everyone else started their careers too, so keep your eye on the prize and do what you are told. Never complain (Q32) and stay enthusiastic (Q11) at all times.

✓ *Be hungry for work.* Offer to take on work. Look for ways to be helpful, even if it's by stuffing envelopes, answering the telephone, or doing the photocopying. Especially when others shun unsexy work, you can demonstrate your can-do attitude and sense of team play.

✓ *Seek feedback on your mistakes.* Every time you complete any reasonably significant task, quiz people for feedback. More specifically, ask for constructive criticism about what you could have done better to not only learn and improve, but also show your bosses that you are willing to learn and improve.

✓ *Focus not only on tasks, but also relationships.* Unless you are training to be a rocket scientist or brain surgeon, you will find that technical expertise alone is not enough to get ahead. Completing tasks and delivering results is only a part of the equation for success; making people warm to you, like you, and want to work with you again is just as important.

Like I said: the rules aren't difficult to understand. The tough bit comes in applying them slavishly. Look around you at the number of your colleagues who do not live by the rules – for example they moan or assume they're doing okay without seeking feedback. They understand the rules intellectually but think they don't apply to them. Make sure you don't fall into that same trap – because these rules apply to everyone.

When you begin
your career, you have
no rights, no privileges.

40 How can I survive the dreaded annual appraisal?

Few bosses use appraisals to good effect. If they have to choose between developing themselves and developing you, which do you think they are more likely to put the effort into? Consequently, the yearly appraisal process is often little more than a bureaucratic chore for both boss and subordinate, involving much paperwork and little useful discussion.

Don't let that be the case for you. It is *your* responsibility to put in some thought to get the most from your appraisal. Rather than viewing it as a tedious trial of your patience, look at it as a session in which you can persuade your boss to support you in achieving your career goals. Use the following guidelines to get the most from your appraisal:

✓ *Consider the value you have added.* How will you "prove" that you have done a good job in the last year? Your boss probably has many appraisals to complete and may simply forget about some of your achievements; it's up to you to bring to mind your successes so that you can remind your boss of them.

Proving that you are a valuable asset to the team may be especially important if your appraisal is linked to bonus payments or pay rises.

✓ *Protect your personal brand.* Your personal brand is how others (including your boss) see you (see also Q94). What do you know that you haven't done so well? How will you explain your actions and make yourself appear in the best possible light? However, avoid becoming defensive when listening to any constructive criticism your boss may have for you (Q43).

✓ *Look to the future.* Think about your personal long-term goals. What skills and experiences are you looking to develop within this organization?

✓ *Build your case.* Sure, you may want to work on a sexy project or be given certain opportunities. But why should you expect your boss to support you? In other words, what's in it for your boss? Think of ways in which your enhanced skills and motivation could allow you to contribute even more to the team's goals and make your boss look like a veritable star.

> # Bring to mind your successes so that you can remind your boss of them.

41 Does anyone really listen to negative feedback?

If your career is a journey, then feedback is your GPS, providing you with information about where you are and how much further you are from your ultimate destination. Feedback tells you whether you are off course and need to channel your energies in a different direction.

Sitting around waiting for feedback is a dangerous career strategy. In fact it's not really a strategy at all. Unless you have a good sense of the level of your skills and performance, you cannot know whether you are making progress towards your goals. Generally speaking, most people hate to give negative feedback. Even when they are asked for it, they may be reluctant to give accurate feedback. No one likes to stick their neck out and be the bearer of bad news. As such, most feedback simply plays back what they think you want to hear as opposed to telling you what you need to hear.

Many people discount criticism when they receive it. They think, "What do you know?" or "You weren't there – you can't understand

> # Praise may make you feel good, but criticism will help you achieve your goals.

why I had to behave that way!" or "You've got the wrong end of the stick." But that's not a strategy for career success either.

I have also met people who can genuinely not recall the last time they received any negative feedback. Which is not to say that they aren't making mistakes or being criticized behind their backs by their colleagues – only that they are not bothering to ask the right questions to find out what they could be doing better.

If you want to get better at what you do, make sure to dig a little deeper. Praise may make you feel good, but criticism will help you achieve your goals.

42 What's the best way to get constructive feedback?

Given most people's intense reluctance to give feedback, you must make it as easy as possible for them to tell you what they really think:

✓ *Plan the questions you wish to ask.* Before you seek feedback from others, know what to ask for. There is no point asking questions about skills that don't matter to you. Think about your vision and long-term goals (Q14) and think about the particular areas of skill that you most need to develop and therefore need feedback on. Prepare both open-ended questions to prompt broad comments and more specific questions to address particular concerns.

✓ *Give adequate notice.* Of course your performance may be foremost in your mind, but other people have other concerns to be getting on with. Explain that you would like to get some feedback not only on what you do well but especially what you could do better, your weaknesses, and any mistakes you may have made. Encourage people to recall specific incidents and occasions to talk through when you meet up.

✓ *Assure people that you will not become defensive.* People's reluctance to give negative feedback often stems from having experienced angry reactions to it. Tell people that you genuinely want to hear negative feedback to understand what you could do better. Reassure them that you want their honest opinion, and will not under any circumstances try to argue or justify yourself (see also Q43).

✓ *Lead the discussion.* As you have asked for feedback, you should set the agenda and lead the meeting. Let people know which areas of your performance you would most like to discuss.

✓ *Show your appreciation.* Offer your sincere thanks to others for having taken the time to help you.

3 How can I deflect criticism?

I'm afraid deflecting criticism is never a good idea. Whether you were at fault or someone misread your behavior, you must accept that someone who has an opinion of you – whether right or wrong – will treat you differently because of it. And that goes irrespectively of how much you may agree or disagree with the criticism.

As such, you must welcome criticism and explore it. And, to get the most from it, mull over the following pointers:

✓ *Respond sensitively.* Remember that most people hate to be perceived as being critical, so you know that it may have taken some courage for them to speak up. Thank other people for poking you in the eye.

✓ *Avoid becoming defensive.* When you receive feedback, your initial response may be to want to stand up for yourself and challenge it. However, defensiveness is a surefire way to cut off future feedback that could otherwise be helping you to achieve your goals. Avoid arguing, justifying yourself, or trying to debate what is being said. Instead, say that you respect their right to an opinion and apologize for any mistakes you may have made if necessary. If you find yourself starting to offer an explanation, stop yourself immediately, as that too will probably be seen as a sign of defensiveness.

✓ *Rein in your tone of voice and body language.* Even if you manage to avoid arguing or attempting to justify your behavior, be careful to check your manner to avoid conveying even a hint of irritation or unhappiness.

✓ *Explore the feedback with questions.* If you do not understand what the other person means, feel free to probe for appropriate examples. Again, however, make sure that your questions genuinely shed light on the feedback, and are not seen as defensive posturing or a challenge to the feedback.

✓ *Think twice about sharing your point of view.* Only share your point of view if the other person expresses an interest in hearing it. Otherwise it will be perceived again only as a form of defensiveness.

✓ *Reflect on the implications of the feedback.* Even if you do not agree with the message of the feedback, ask yourself how the other person came to misunderstand a situation or misread your behavior (see also Q45 on learning from regular reflection). If the feedback is correct, consider what lessons you can learn from it (see also Q44 on developing yourself and Q35 on managing your weaknesses).

> # Thank other people for poking you in the eye.

4 How can I learn and develop myself?

Anyone can pull together a self-improvement plan. The question is whether you have the motivation to follow it through. Being told by your boss to work on some area of skill or knowledge is rarely inducement enough. Having a vision (Q13) of what you want to achieve in your career and life, and the knowledge that your self-improvement plan will help you to turn your vision into reality – now that's motivation.

To stand the best chance of creating a successful self-improvement plan, consider the following guidelines:

✓ *Select only a small number of development goals.* It is better to make progress on a few core skills, behaviors, or areas of knowledge than spread your efforts so thinly that your learning does not get embedded. Choose to work on only two or three high-priority areas in which you can make the most difference in achieving your vision. You can always add more activities to your plan once you have achieved your initial goals.

✓ *Devise a concrete action plan.* In the same way that organizations devise business plans for guiding them towards important goals, think about your plan in terms of action steps, people or other resources you may need to involve, timeframes, and so on (see also Q17 on setting SPORTY goals). You are the only person who will see the plan, so devise a format that you will actually use.

✓ *Take small steps.* You are more likely to embed new knowledge and behavior if you learn in tiny, incremental, bite-sized chunks than if you aim to do all your learning in a single marathon session. Ideally, commit to engage in some activity every day (see also Q45). Consider a mix of activities such as observing colleagues and role models, trying the skill out, reading, attending seminars or workshops, and talking to experts.

✓ *Be prepared for discomfort.* Be patient and realize that sustainable change takes time. You may feel unwieldy using a new skill or applying an area of knowledge for quite some time until it becomes properly embedded in your repertoire. In fact, feeling self-conscious and awkward at first is a good sign – at least you know that you're moving beyond your comfort zone.

✓ *Elicit frequent feedback.* Seek feedback when you are not sure of your progress (Q41). However, be careful not to obsess over feedback and pester colleagues for feedback after every little task you complete.

> # Learn in tiny, incremental, bite-sized chunks.

45 How else can I accelerate my self-development?

Q44 covered putting together a self-improvement plan of actions that will help you move towards your goals. But action is of little use if it is the wrong action.

Effective development requires not only action but also reflection. I realize that sitting in quiet thought may not feel very dynamic and thrusting, but that's exactly the point. Rather than rushing around expending energy doing, doing, doing, take the time to think occasionally. High-achievers pause to reflect on the appropriateness of their actions, understand what behaviors are paying off, and discard activities that don't work as part of a continuing drive to become more effective. Reflection is about thinking – you don't want to be thoughtless do you?

You don't have to overcomplicate reflection. Simply find the time occasionally to ask yourself four basic questions:

1. What have I done recently that was successful?

2. Given my successes, what must I continue to do in the future?

3. What have I done recently that didn't work so well?

4. Given my mistakes or misadventures, what must I do differently in the future?

> # Action is of little use if it is the wrong action.

To make the most of your reflection:

✓ *Create a regular time for reflection.* Consider integrating reflection into your list of priorities for each day or week (for example making it a 'box 2' activity – see Q27). Reflect on your progress over different time frames – a day, a week, a month, a seven-month project. Mix up the time frames over which you reflect to see if you can distil lessons that weren't apparent nearer the time.

✓ *Consider keeping a journal.* Reflecting during your daily commute to work or while doing the ironing may save you time, but consider whether it's the most effective way to learn from it. Scribbling your thoughts on paper every so often is likely to be more productive – especially given the power of writing down goals (see Q25).

✓ *Invest effort in your reflection.* No development activity should ever feel routine. Asking yourself the same few questions is likely to dull the benefits over time. Think of new questions to quiz yourself occasionally. For example, rather than always asking yourself about your own performance, consider what you could learn from other people. Who impressed you recently? What specifically did he or she say or do? What could you learn from him or her or adapt for your own behavioral repertoire?

46 What's the best way to deal with organizational change?

It's human nature to resist change. If something has been working well, why change it? Even if something isn't working well, how can we know if the alternative will be any better?

Most people are reluctant to take on board change at work. But change is an undeniable part of life and our work. Barely 20 years ago, we didn't have the Internet, mobile phones, globalization, computers in every home, Starbucks coffee shops on every street corner, any awareness of the threat of climate change, iPods – the list goes on. And as technology and society move on, so must organizations.

Resisting organizational change is foolish. The world continues to change and a refusal to get on board will leave you behind. Of course it's understandable that many of the changes in your organization may make you feel uncomfortable. Perhaps your organization wishes you to take on different or more responsibilities or land you with a new, nightmarish boss. Perhaps your organization wishes to cull the size of your budget, restructure your team, move its head office to another city or country, even make you redundant. However, resisting change is not a viable career strategy.

The only bulletproof route to job security is through building a unique portfolio of skills and experiences. It's better to assume that change will happen rather than hope that it doesn't and end up disappointed.

Much of the change that occurs around us will mean that circumstances are genuinely beyond our control. But even if you can't control what happens to you, *you can control how you respond to a situation*. Even if we are victims of terrible circumstances, we can choose to either feel aggrieved and spend our time grumbling, or take action to improve the situation. Having a long-term vision (Q13) means that you can more easily decide how to react to any immediate changes that are going on around you, no matter how sudden and unexpected they may be.

Whether you are 16 years old or 61 years old, never resign yourself to believing that it is too late to change. I coached an entrepreneur

> # The world continues to change and a refusal to get on board will leave you behind.

last year who, at the age of 61, having developed but subsequently recovered from a life-threatening illness, was preparing to embark on a new business venture. Whatever your age, you can take control of your career so that you no longer have to worry about the changes that your organization may decide to impose on you.

47 Why should I network?

If success at work fundamentally comes down to people (Q1), it makes sense to get out, meet more people, build more relationships.

I'm coaching an investment banker at the moment in his late 20s. He has been observing with amazement the networking efforts of one of his peers, a Canadian. The Canadian has different black books filled with notes on the people he has met. Every day he flicks through his books, picks up the telephone, and invites people for drinks after work on most evenings, and for lunch at least two or three times a week. Rather than get bogged down in the day-to-day demands of his punishing job, he has prioritized the "people stuff." Not surprisingly he's one of the youngest vice presidents at the bank.

Especially when it comes to finding opportunities to do gorgeous and exciting work, it helps if people know you exist, can remember what you're good at, and like you too. Managers can be quite lazy when it comes time to promote people or put them on sexy projects; they often look no further than the cozy clump of people they know well. It doesn't matter how good you are if the right people do not think of you (see also Q75).

Networks also allow you to make things happen. Often, our ability to reach organizational objectives is decided by other people. When people are busy, they will of course respond more willingly to requests for help from people they know and like than people who are strangers to them. Neither should you neglect the power of networks for generating ideas. On average, the more you talk to people, the more likely you are to discover good ideas and occasionally truly brilliant ones that could make a huge difference to your career. You can never tell when it might happen. But get away from your desk to talk to two or three times as many people and you double or triple your chances.

> # No one likes to feel used; if you are a phoney, you will give yourself away.

Despite the benefits of networking, many people feel that it is inappropriate for them. Perhaps they feel uncomfortable about the prospect of having to schmooze and faking interest. But let's get one point clear straightaway. Effective networking is not about pretending to like people, being solely self-interested, brown-nosing, kissing ass, sucking up, or being insincere. Human beings have remarkably sophisticated bullshit detection systems – we can subconsciously detect people's intentions through their body language and tone of voice very accurately. No one likes to feel used; if you are a phoney, you will give yourself away.

48 What's the secret to effective networking?

Effective networking must fundamentally focus on building mutually beneficial relationships with other people. Shameless networking that focuses only on your self-interest quickly closes doors. Here are some guidelines for effective networking:

✓ *Focus on mutual interest.* Find something that you have in common with the people you want to connect with. You could build the relationship on mutual either professional or personal interests, but the most effective relationships combine both. For example, if you have a sporting interest in common, stir up a friendly rivalry between your team and theirs. If you both have children of a similar age or are yourselves single and dating, use that to reinforce what you have in common. Such interests do not have to be big and clever – they only need to connect the two of you in some way.

✓ *Decide how explicitly you wish to discuss benefits.* There may be certain individuals with whom you feel comfortable openly asking for help in return for some form of assistance or support that you can offer. With others, especially those who may have little interest in the professional benefits of staying in touch with you, you may need to foster more of a personal and social relationship.

✓ *Focus on quality, not quantity.* Yes you could grow your network by working a room at a conference or other professional event, handing out business cards to every stranger you meet. But would you be able to call upon those people for support and advice? Effective networking is not a cut-and-run activity. Having superficial conversations that merely gather names into your database is not networking – don't do it.

✓ *Focus on the relationship, not the career benefit from it.* If you manage to do the former, the latter takes care of itself. If you focus on what you can get out of someone, you can say goodbye to the relationship. Unless you have a relationship that explicitly recognizes the mutual career benefits, try to think of networking as building relationships with new friends rather than with people who could be useful to you.

> # Having superficial conversations that merely gather names into your database is not networking – don't do it.

49 What's the best way to kick off my networking campaign?

While effective networking is always based on *mutual benefit*, there is no reason you cannot also be strategic and methodical in building your network. Use the following steps to guide your efforts:

1. *Map your network.* Sketch a diagram of your existing network that encompasses everyone within your organization that you know. Include both lateral links (i.e. those with peers in other teams or departments) as well as vertical links (i.e. those with individuals both senior and junior to you). Write next to their names the ways in which you can help them and vice versa.

2. *Identify your needs.* Consider your long-term goals and ask yourself what you are trying to get out of your network. Look at your networking map and think about the gaps within it. Who would you like to add to your network?

3. *Consider what you can offer.* In this most critical step, ask yourself what you can offer people in terms of information, ideas, resources, or influence. If there is no professional reason for

you to get in touch, consider how you could build the relationship based more on social or personal interests. Whatever the case, make sure you have something to offer, and work out at least broadly how you will introduce yourself and explain your reasons for getting in touch.

4. *Develop a plan for initiating contact.* Find a way to get in touch. If you already know them, consider dropping by their desk or inviting them for a coffee, lunch, or drink after work. If you don't know them, consider who in your network could introduce you. Volunteering to work on cross-functional projects is also a good way to meet different colleagues (see also Q39).

5. *Identify the right times to network.* Make it a priority to attend social events organized by your employer. It's often the lunches, dinners, and drinks preceding or following formal events that are the most fertile times for networking with peers and people more senior to yourself.

> # Ask yourself what you can offer people in terms of information, ideas, resources, or influence.

50 How can I deepen relationships within my network?

Making first contact with someone is a start. But effective networks are based on deep relationships of trust and understanding. Trust and understanding can't be forced – they take time to develop. So take your time. Aim to strengthen the depth of your relationships over the course of many months by following these pointers:

✓ *Look for ways to be supportive.* The more you help people, the more positively predisposed toward you they will become. There are practical forms of support such as offering your time, ideas, advice, access to other people you know, and influence. However, you can also be supportive by listening to their problems, showing your interest or concern, and simply being a fun person to be around.

✓ *Keep in touch regularly.* Unsurprisingly, someone who only hears from you when you need a favor may suspect your motives and be more than a little reluctant to help. So make an effort to stay in touch *before* you have need to do so. Keeping in touch with key contacts may never be urgent, but is often important (see Q26). Develop your own rituals and routines (e.g. fire off a dozen emails every Sunday afternoon, send postcards to people you meet, meet a colleague for lunch every Tuesday and a customer for breakfast every other Monday) so that networking becomes an integral part of your behavior.

✓ *Be authentic.* People can spot fakes a mile away. You can pretend to have an interest in any topic for a short period of time, but may struggle to sustain such efforts successfully over a longer stretch of time. If someone you know is a football fan and you have no such interest, figuring out the right questions to ask while at the same time fending off questions that could show up your lack of knowledge in the area will be difficult in the extreme. Look for common ground in areas in which you have a genuine interest too.

✓ *Reciprocate.* Relationships that involve give-and-take tend to be stronger than ones in which the support goes mainly one-way. If you are always helping another person and never asking for help, the relationship can become unbalanced; the other person may feel indebted to you and become less likely to come to you for support. Ensure that you exchange support rather than simply providing assistance and banking lots of favors until you need a big favor returned.

> # People can spot fakes a mile away.

51 How can I extend my network?

A large network of superficial contacts is not really a network at all, so make sure you first develop the existing relationships that you already have (Q50). Consider these suggestions for extending your network, particularly outside of your organization:

✓ *Develop your slogan.* Possibly the first question people ask each other when they meet is "What do you do?" Prepare a "blurb" or verbal logo that allows you to introduce yourself in straightforward and interesting terms to anyone, no matter what their background. Choose no more than 50 words to captivate interest rather than simply repeating your actual job description. Think about what is exciting, sexy, or quirky about your job or background to bring a smile to people's faces and get them wanting to know more. Write your slogan out, practice it, try it on friends and family. There's no need to confuse people with industry-specific language or jargon (see Q77) so keep it simple and in plain English too.

✓ *Take an active role in industry or professional associations.* Look at your long-term career vision (Q13) and decide what kinds of people you want to meet. Investigate workshops, seminars, meetings, and conferences that would give you exposure to such individuals. If you can, look for opportunities to speak at events, as it gives you license to approach nearly anyone in the audience.

✓ *Decide on the networking approach that works for you.* Some networkers advocate flitting around a room, spending no more than five or ten minutes with each person before gathering their card up and moving on. However, that approach works only if you possess superb networking skills and can build genuine rapport within only minutes. Playing social butterfly may allow you to meet more people, but you must ensure that when you get in touch with them again, you are able to demonstrate some genuine interest in them to turn that superficial contact into a proper relationship. Personally, I don't enjoy "working a room" so I'm more likely to chat to fewer people for much longer, which results in a smaller number of slightly deeper initial contacts. Choose whichever tactic works for you best.

52 Any final tips on effective networking?

I've said it already but I'll say it again: networking is a big deal. Sure, you could try to get ahead without networking, but then again you could also try to get ahead by putting in 16-hour days, seven days a week.

To become a consummate master or mistress of networking, be sure to:

✓ *Network in all directions.* Novice networkers often try too hard to ingratiate themselves with senior people. However, seeking to network with people who are very much more senior may be problematic if you have neither professional or personal interests in common. It is often easier to begin networking with peers and others at a similar level because they will at least tend to have similar work and possibly life experiences. Make an effort with support staff and people who are junior to you too – they do move on and may become useful contacts in other organizations.

✓ *Keep track of your network.* Devise a simple system for jotting down notes on both the professional and personal lives of the people you come across. Being able to enquire about a contact's family by their names or remembering that someone had just moved house the last time you spoke to him or her will make others warm to you again more quickly.

✓ *Prioritize your network.* In practice you will meet some people who could be more useful to you than others. Going through your list of contacts and highlighting an A-list of people allows you to decide how best to spend your limited time keeping in touch with them. This does not need to be a lengthy or Machiavellian process. Simply flick through your address book and ask yourself who you really should get in touch with again.

✓ *Maintain your network.* Don't become so mired in your day-to-day work that you believe yourself too "busy" to network. Send the occasional email, meet for an occasional drink or sandwich, arrange an annual dinner with a group of like-minded contacts, invite people to a share a quick coffee and croissant before work. Spending time with your network makes the difference between having lots of names in your little black book and having a network of useful relationships.

For further pointers on using your network, see also Q84.

> # Don't become so mired in your day-to-day work that you believe yourself too "busy" to network.

How important is intelligence in determining career success?

You don't need to be clever to succeed – at least not in the traditional, measured by IQ, kind of way. In simpler times, there used to be a much bigger advantage for people who were academically gifted, smart, or clever. But such advantages have gradually been eroded over the years.

I'm sure you know stories of entrepreneurs – including icons such as Michael Dell and Richard Branson – who struggled at school or dropped out of university. Conventional education had all but given up on them, but they went on to do fairly well, didn't they?

In fact, experience suggests that people who may have done very well at school or university often struggle the most when they enter the workforce. They have been so used to being top of the class for their academic brilliance and exam performance that they arrive into the workforce with a sense of entitlement, and imagine career progression will be handed to them on a plate. They expect only challenging, exciting work and may be contemptuous of work that appears menial. Such individuals often end up having their

> # Success more often depends on relationships than knowing the square root of 259.

careers cut short by bosses who perceive them to have "attitude problems."

Success more often depends on relationships than knowing the square root of 259. People who are intellectually gifted often succeed only in technical or specialist roles. It's the people who have the broader people skills – emotional intelligence, if you will – who succeed in broader occupations such as becoming good managers, sales people, entrepreneurs, consultants, and leaders. So don't sweat it if you didn't get straight As at school because investing effort in relationships is all that really counts.

54 What else could I do if I'm not classed as traditionally "intelligent"?

Most corporate-y organizations are dull, dull, dull. They all basically do the same thing – take money from customers, clients or consumers, make products or services, and sell them. Like I said: dull.

And in their incredibly dull ways, they look to hire people with dull verbal and numerical sorts of skills. But there are other types of intelligence that can lead to success too. Drawing upon three decades of research, Howard Gardner, a professor at the Harvard Graduate School of Education, has suggested that there may actually be eight distinct types of intelligence or "smarts":

✓ *Linguistic "word smart."* Talents in reading, writing, listening, and communicating through words.

✓ *Logical-mathematical "number/reasoning smart."* An aptitude for performing calculations, analyzing puzzles and solving logical problems.

✓ *Spatial "picture smart."* A gift for knowing your orientation (e.g. location and direction) in space and knowing how to move from one location to another, such as reading maps or orienteering.

✓ *Bodily-kinaesthetic "body smart."* Talents to do with using your body or a part of your body (e.g. your hands) to perform skilful and purposeful movements, as sculptors, surgeons, or dancers might.

✓ *Musical "music smart."* Aptitude for playing, singing, and composing.

✓ *Interpersonal "people smart."* A gift for understanding others and your relationships with them (see also Q56 on emotional intelligence).

✓ *Intrapersonal "self smart."* A flair for understanding yourself and having insight into your own thoughts, emotions, and actions (see also Q56).

✓ *Naturalistic "nature smart."* An ability to work in the natural world with animals and other living things.

Traditional education has focused almost exclusively on the first two types of "smarts." Many organizations hire specifically for those narrow skills, and are perhaps only now beginning to realize the importance of the interpersonal and intrapersonal smarts. But there's a whole world of opportunities outside of even those types of intelligence.

If those traditional types of intelligence are not where your strengths lie, you will have to invest a lot of time and effort to become merely adequate in what does not come naturally to you. Why not focus instead on areas that do come naturally? Sure, it may take you away from the more conventional career paths of corporate life, but wouldn't it be worth it to become great or even truly extraordinary (see also Q34)?

5 Do I need an MBA?

Business schools often promise rich rewards in terms of pay, promotion, and prestige for MBA students. But an MBA is not an automatic guarantee of career success. In fact, I once met someone at my gym who had been lured from abroad to do an MBA. He was working at the snack bar making cappuccinos and toasting bagels for 18 months, such was the worth of his MBA – I won't mention the name of the business school he graduated from.

Before you sign on the dotted line to pay the usually very hefty fees to do an MBA, consider some of these guidelines:

✓ *Be clear on your career goals.* Analyze what you hope to gain from an MBA that you could not get any other way, for example by taking a secondment, moving into a new role in a different organization for a few years, taking a sabbatical, seeking particular project work, offering to work for free for the right organization for a few months to gain relevant experience, and so on. Look for people within your organization or your broader network who have careers and lives like the one you would like to have. Find out whether attending business school was a key plank of their success or whether they managed it in any other way.

✓ *Beware the hype.* Not all business schools are created equally. Given the amounts of money to be made from MBA students, all business schools talk up their credentials. A survey earlier this year by top executive search firm Egon Zehnder found that only one in five international managers believed that an MBA prepares people to deal with the real-life challenges that a manager has to face. Put another way, 80 percent of managers thought an MBA doesn't prepare you for business in the real world.

✓ *Do your own independent research.* Seek headhunters and other people within your network to get an independent perspective on the reputation of any particular business school you are seriously considering. Figure out what they consider the main benefits of gaining an MBA. If success more often comes down to who you know than what you know (Q1), are you 100 percent sure an MBA is right for you?

56 Does emotional intelligence really matter?

Emotional intelligence – sometimes called EQ – matters for two reasons. First, your organization believes it's important for becoming customer-focused and a great leader. And when an organization starts to believe in the importance of a quality, it frequently starts to measure it. If you don't display such skills – irrespective of whether you believe in their importance or not – you could get held up in your climb up the career ladder.

Second, research and experience tells us that emotional intelligence distinguishes between winners and also-rans. Whether your goals are to become a rich entrepreneur or a popular leader, a manager who delivers results or someone who successfully juggles work and home, a growing body of evidence points to the fact that emotional intelligence can make a critical difference.

While the term "emotional intelligence" may smack of the latest fad, it is merely a currently fashionable label for what people have known for decades, namely that people skills count (Q1).

But what is emotional intelligence exactly? EQ broadly covers three broad skill areas, none of which should strike you as new or unexpected:

✓ *Self- and social awareness.* The foundation of emotional intelligence is being able to identify moods and emotions in ourselves and understand how these affect other people. Many people are blind to the true impact that they have on others. In much the same way as the vast majority of people believe themselves to have above-average senses of humor, driving skills, and abilities to please their lovers in bed, many of us are not fully aware of our impact on others (see also Q94 on personal branding).

✓ *Self-direction.* People who self-direct can identify their own emotions and how they affect others, and also change those emotions when necessary. Having an awareness that you are angry, frightened, or unhappy is a start. But the truly emotionally intelligent can discipline their emotions, choosing to calm their frustrations, soothe away their fears, and stimulate enthusiasm when they need to.

✓ *Interpersonal savvy.* The pinnacle of emotional intelligence is being able to manage emotional states in other people, to appease their resentment or motivate them when they feel down. Interpersonal savvy is essentially the skill of figuring out what makes other people tick; it is discovering other people's buttons so you can push them.

> # Emotional intelligence distinguishes between winners and also-rans.

57 So how can I sharpen my emotional intelligence?

While the term "emotional intelligence" may suggest that EQ (like IQ) is an innate quality you are either born with or without, the good news is that EQ is actually a set of skills that can be taught and developed, much like any other skill. So no matter how easy or difficult you find the skills of dealing with others, you can improve and get even better at them by using the following techniques:

✓ *Examine your own emotions.* Enhance your self-awareness by reflecting on your moods and emotions. In the same way that you and your colleagues might periodically review lessons learned from a project or client account, make time to review your own feelings. What events made you feel a certain way? How did those feelings then influence your behavior? How could you in future dampen down unhelpful emotions or help yourself to bring about more useful ones? Writing about your feelings in a journal may give you greater insight into your feelings and therefore how to control them (see also Q45).

✓ *Try mind-reading.* Develop your empathy by peering into

the mind of the people you work with. Pick one person at a time and replay in your mind the behavior and the emotions that person displays. Figure out what motivates, distresses, bores, or relaxes that person. Study the person until you can build a picture of his/her ambitions, passions, likes, and dislikes, and can predict the person's reactions in different situations. The more you scrutinize the behavior and likely thoughts of others, the better you will become at understanding and therefore influencing them.

✓ *Put the theory into practice.* Reflecting on your own emotions and those of others is an important first step; however, remember that others judge us on what we *do*, not what we *think*. Talk through unpleasant or awkward people situations with colleagues or mentors, seek feedback on your behavior, and look for ways to integrate new habits and behaviors to do with how you display your emotions and interact with others in your day-to-day work (see Q44 on developing skills).

58 How can you change someone's behavior?

OK, we all work with people who don't pull their weight. But before you wade into a confrontation to give a difficult colleague the benefit of your advice, consider that your words will almost certainly fall on deaf ears.

You've probably experienced this phenomenon yourself. Perhaps you're not so good at something at home – perhaps a partner, parent or roommate keeps reminding you to take the rubbish out, clean the bath, or tidy up a bit more. While you may eventually change your behavior, you probably hate their nit picking and nagging, their badgering and pestering. And, given half a chance, you would probably go back to your bad habits.

Criticizing others wounds their sense of pride and puts them on the defensive. Even when criticism is sensitively phrased and made with the best intentions, it can stir up feelings of resentment rather than acting as any real incentive to change.

Oddly enough, the way to change people's behavior is not to point out what they do *wrong*, but to focus on what they do *right*. Many decades ago, a renowned animal psychologist by the name of B. F. Skinner discovered that rewarding an animal for good behavior was a far more effective way of changing its behavior than punishing it for bad behavior. Despite what we may like to believe, we humans are all still animals – albeit highly evolved animals. Praising and recognizing what a colleague does well is a more effective inducement to changing his or her behavior than criticizing what he or she does wrong.

Suppose one of your colleagues repeatedly – and frustratingly for you – forgets to write up the minutes from various meetings. Well, on the rare occasion that your colleague does remember to do them (even if they need reminding to do so), praise his or her behavior. Thank your colleague genuinely, explain how it helps you or the rest of the team out, and show your appreciation. Don't layer the flattery on too thickly, but praise it nonetheless. And the same goes for the next time your colleague remembers to do it. It may take weeks or months, but gradually you will notice your colleague becoming more diligent with those meeting minutes. It's not quite hey presto – but you've changed your colleague's behavior.

> # Criticizing others wounds their sense of pride and puts them on the defensive.

59 How can you repair a relationship that has broken down?

The best way to restore a relationship is to learn to recognize an individual's strengths. In much the same way as we can help ourselves to succeed by focusing on our strengths rather than dwelling on our weaknesses (Q34), you can often build relationships more successfully by focusing quite deliberately on that individual's strengths and not his or her faults. Follow these guidelines to defuse tension and get your relationship back on track:

✓ *Figure out the individual's strengths.* Over the course of several weeks, identify what it is that other colleagues value about this person. Keep observing his or her interactions with others until you are able to write down a list of at least five of the individual's positive skills or traits.

✓ *Show your appreciation for the individual's strengths.* Whenever you work with the individual, keep these strengths at the forefront of your mind and draw attention to what the person does well. Make positive comments on the individual's skills or qualities when it is appropriate to do so. But offer your thanks, compliments and praise only when you feel it is genuinely deserved; otherwise you will sound false and simply worsen the situation.

✓ *Avoid making any negative comments.* Remember your objective is to show your appreciation for the person's strengths and restore the relationship. The time for giving constructive criticism will come only much, much later when you have established a strong working relationship.

✓ *Avoid complaining about the person to third parties.* Be careful not to mention your frustrations to others, as your comments could easily be relayed back to the individual and destroy the precious trust you may have built up.

As the weeks and months go by, you will find it easier to overlook the qualities that once made your relationship difficult. Not only will you find yourself warming to the other person – at first grudgingly and perhaps even against your will – but you may find that individual becoming more gracious and affable to you too. You don't believe me that it works? Keep track of the number of positive comments you make each time you work with the individual; in turn, make a note of how many positive comments you get back in return. Over time, watch the tally of mutual comments grow. Trust me, it works.

50 What's the best way to give constructive criticism?

First of all, consider that praising what someone does right is often a better way to retrain that person's behavior than pointing out what he or she is doing wrong (see Q58). Having said that, there may be occasions when someone is badly off-track or could clearly benefit from you speaking up about what the individual is doing wrong.

Always give criticism in private so as not to embarrass someone in front of others. Remember also that constructive criticism should aim to change behavior, not prove that you were right. Finally, ensure that your feedback obeys the "seven Cs" of effective criticism:

✓ *Clear.* Prepare what you want to say ahead of time to ensure you can explain the detail of the situation exactly as you observed it.

✓ *Current.* Give feedback as soon after an event as possible so that all parties can recall the details well enough to learn from them.

✓ *Candid.* Being honest should go both ways – both you and the individual should feel able to talk openly about your interpretation of events. It could even transpire that you had misunderstood something or made a mistake that contributed to the other person's situation. If you have more experience, authority, or seniority than the other person, make sure he or she feels able to speak up without fear of reprisal.

✓ *Consequential.* Explain the impact of the individual's behavior. Saying "You speak too loudly on the telephone" is not as compelling as explaining "You speak too loudly on the telephone, which means that the people working next to you can't work productively."

✓ *Confidence-building.* Aim is to build someone up, not tear them down. Help the individual to consider the criticism in the broader context of what he or she does right. Aim to bolster the person's mood and confidence as much as to point out exactly what he or she did wrong.

✓ *Constructive.* Rather than simply pointing out what the other person did wrong, make sure you can offer suggestions as to how the situation could be handled differently next time. If it's appropriate, you could also ask what support you could offer to help the individual to improve.

✓ *Consistent.* Ensure you give feedback to whoever might need it. Be careful not to overlook the shortcomings of people who happen to be your friends as it will damage the atmosphere within the team.

> # Criticism should aim to change behavior, not prove that you were right.

61 How can I defuse conflict at work?

Conflict is an inevitable consequence of working with other people who may be competing for limited resources or who may have different responsibilities, priorities, or points of view.

The problem with conflict is when it gets personal – when people start to blame each other rather than look for a solution. Consequently, the best way to defuse conflict is to ignore whatever may have caused the situation in the first place. Accept that there may have been someone or something that triggered it all off, but start from the perspective that whatever caused the conflict is no longer important. It's ancient history. The only thing that matters is to find a solution, discussing *how* to solve the conflict rather than *why* the conflict arose. Try working through these steps:

1. *Set the scene.* Arrange a private meeting with the other person and explain that you want to find a solution. Stress that you're willing to compromise, and express the hope that he or she is too. Most good solutions require compromises from both parties rather than allowing one person to "win" and the other to "lose."

2. *Understand the other person's perspective.* Ask lots of questions and use active listening skills (Q65) to look at what's not

working, rather than who is to blame. Posing questions and allowing the other person to talk and vent his or her frustrations will boost your chances of reaching a settlement. But keep the tone of the discussion positive – if you find it starts to get heated, suggest taking a break to cool off.

3. *Brainstorm and evaluate options.* Once you have isolated what's not working, suggest brainstorming collaboratively to identify possible solutions. Remember that your focus should be on how to manage the situation rather than why it came about. When you have come up with at least a handful of alternatives, work together to weigh up the pros and cons of each.

4. *Commit to a solution.* Finally, identify the solution that has the most benefits and fewest drawbacks. Then work to agree action steps, assign responsibilities, decide on timescales for completion, and so on.

You can't make conflict go away. Whether it's down to a lack of resources, differences in personal agendas, or any other reason, it's unlikely that those circumstances will change of their own accord. But by focusing on solutions rather than reasons for the conflict, you can at least achieve part of what you want.

> Focus on *how to* solve the conflict rather than *why* the conflict arose.

What is the best way to deal with interpersonal conflict?

We all know that we should never let things get personal at work. But sometimes we can't help it and things do get personal. And when that happens, boy, can it get bad.

One of the best ways to deal with interpersonal differences is to reinforce someone's strengths (see Q59). However, that approach takes time, and assumes that you have enough of a working relationship to be able to be in the same room at the same time without screaming and shouting at each other.

If you do find yourself in a situation in which the relationship has not so much broken down as collapsed beyond repair, consider the steps in Q61 to find a solution that allows you to work together again. But consider also these additional tips for clearing the air first:

✓ *Make a supreme effort to stay calm.* Watch your tone of voice and body language. Speak more quietly and more slowly than you normally would. Look even at how you use your hands –

be careful to use open-palmed gestures rather than balling them into fists. If you are naturally a passionate person, this may be the most tricky step of all.

✓ *Establish feelings as well as facts.* Encourage your adversary to express not only what he or she thinks, but also feels (see also Q65 on deploying the active listening technique). Pay attention to tone of voice and body language cues too to understand how the person really feels about the situation.

✓ *Express your point of view with care.* Be explicit that, when you talk about what you think and feel, you are expressing only your personal point of view rather than claiming you know the absolute truth of the matter. Use the first person singular (by saying "I") rather than the second person ("you"). For example, saying "You exclude me from meetings" or "You were angry with me" implies that you can read a person's mind about their intentions, when you obviously can't. Statements sound less accusatory when explained from the first person perspective, e.g. "I felt excluded from your meetings" or "I felt that you were angry with me." To reinforce this important difference, you may also wish to preface some of your comments with conciliatory phrases such as "This is only my impression, but I feel..." and "I'm sorry if this isn't correct, but my sense was that..."

I have to admit that handling interpersonal conflict doesn't come easily to me. But adopting these few simple tips has helped me to become much better at it. Try them: they work.

Statements sound less accusatory when explained from the first person perspective.

63 How can I improve my popularity at work?

There is no secret to becoming popular. Ever since Dale Carnegie wrote *How to Win Friends and Influence People* back in 1934, it has been common knowledge what you need to do. Forgive me if the following points sound obvious – I doubt if you or even a single one of your colleagues would be surprised by them. But how many of them live by these rules? Not many, I'll bet. Because the difficulty is typically not in comprehending these suggestions, but *applying* them diligently:

✓ *Exude positivity.* Moods are contagious. Just as we often yawn when we see others yawning, we can spread smiles too. If you are angry or upset, you can bring others down; if you are happy, you can make others feel happy too (see also Q11 on enthusiasm). Even when you don't feel like it, force yourself to perk up – you'll find others being drawn irresistibly toward you.

✓ *Show genuine interest in others.* Most people are more interested in their own hopes and dreams, gripes and upsets than those of anyone else. Demonstrate your interest in others by asking the right questions, and you will find that they may value you above all others.

✓ *Express sincere appreciation for others.* Amazingly, most employees crave more for respect and appreciation than money. People more often quit their jobs because they feel unappreciated than because they need more money. I came across one survey that said that 65 percent of employees had not received any recognition for good work in the last year. Wow. That's quite a lot of disgruntled people. Because we forget to thank others and show how we appreciate them. Make it your priority to demonstrate to others how you value them if you want to be voted Mister or Miss Congeniality (see also Q64).

Many people feel that such behaviors do not come naturally to them; they feel "fake" for adopting them. However, consider that any new skill feels unnatural at first. Driving a car, learning to play golf or a musical instrument – none of these "come naturally" the first time you try them. Any new skill feels awkward for a while. But the more you practice such behaviors, the more quickly they will become part of your natural repertoire (see also Q17 on developing SPORTY goals and Q44 on developing skills).

> # We forget to thank others and show how we appreciate them.

64 How can you offer praise without sounding insincere?

We've established that praise is important (Q63). Trust me when I say that most employees are genuinely starved of recognition and praise. Most of us get so bogged down in our jobs that we forget to show others how we appreciate them. We think of offering praise as a nice-to-have rather than a must-have, and something we'll get round to when we have the time. *Make* the time to do it.

Offering flattery is simple enough. Telling people how good they look or how clever they are is an easy way to compliment them. But people quickly see through such transparent ruses. To be properly effective, praise and recognition must:

✓ *Acknowledge efforts rather than results.* People respond most to feedback that they feel is deserved. As such, praise must recognize their actions and hard work rather than the results that they may or may not have achieved. For example, suppose a sales person gains a new client purely by chance – the individual may even feel slightly embarrassed if you start to commend his or her achievement. However, the same sales person is more likely to appreciate your kind words in acknowledgment of the long hours of research and many meetings he or she put in to try to win a new customer, even if the customer ultimately decided not to buy.

✓ *Be specific.* Vague statements such as "That's a great piece of work" or "Good job on the Henderson account" tend to be less impactful than more specific comments. To make your praise more powerful, describe the precise actions the individual took that merited praise too, e.g. "Spending all that time with the client and building the relationship helped us to get a better understanding of their organization's needs."

✓ *Be individually meaningful.* Praise that is both deserved and specific will live long in your colleagues' memories. However, if you can also make your praise individually meaningful, your words will be remembered forever. We all take pride in different parts of ourselves. While one person might like to be thought of as a mathematical genius, others might find it more rewarding to be seen as having a deep sense of empathy or great presentation skills. Recognizing the particular strengths of people that they themselves value is a surefire way to win them over.

> # Praise that is both deserved and specific will live long in your colleagues' memories.

65 How can I improve my listening skills?

Having good listening skills is a prerequisite for building effective relationships. However, the unvarnished truth is that most people overestimate their listening skills. Whether in groups or when interacting one-on-one, many people spend more time talking than listening. On the other hand, sitting mutely while another person talks at us is not a sign of effective listening either.

Good listeners use a technique called active listening by asking sensitive questions, checking that they understand what is being said, and demonstrating that they are paying attention through a dance of verbal and non-verbal cues. Use these pointers to get the benefits of the technique:

✓ *Give the speaker your full attention.* Make good eye contact and avoid other distractions, such as your computer if you're sitting at your desk, or any notes you may have brought with you to a meeting.

✓ *Use dynamic cues to signal attention.* Lean towards the speaker, nod your head and raise your eyebrows occasionally, and use appropriate facial expressions to demonstrate that you are following the gist of the conversation.

✓ *Ask open-ended questions.* Seek to understand what the speaker is saying by asking questions that begin with words such as "how," "why," "what," and "when." Avoid asking closed questions, i.e. questions that can only be answered with a "yes" or "no," as they try to snatch control of the conversation from the person you are listening to. For example, asking, "Did you feel upset by that?" could be inappropriate if a person was either clearly upset by it ("Yes, of course I was upset, haven't you been listening?") or plainly not upset by it ("No, why should I have been upset by it?"). A better question in that situation may be: "How did you feel about that?"

✓ *Avoid interrupting the speaker.* Speak only when you're sure the person you're listening to has finished talking. It's better to allow the occasional silence to develop than risk inadvertently talking over people. And of course avoid finishing off the other person's sentences as that conveys the impression of impatience.

✓ *Paraphrase what is being said.* Periodically summarize in your own words what you think the speaker is telling you with phrases such as "What you seem to be saying is that ..." and "As I understand it, you ..." Doing so ensures that you have understood correctly what is being said and allows the speaker to correct any misunderstanding on your part.

> The unvarnished truth
> is that many people
> overestimate their
> own listening skills.

66 How can I deal with a difficult colleague?

People are rarely intentionally difficult. More often, people experience difficulties when their values or personalities don't match. We talk about having personality differences or personality clashes with people, but let's consider what they mean in practice.

Personality essentially describes our preferences: how we like to take in information, deal with people, organize our lives, and so on. Take the case of "extroverts" and "introverts." Extroverts like to be around other people; they prefer to talk through ideas rather than read about them; they like to solve problems through discussion with other people. Introverts, on the other hand, prefer their own company; they prefer to receive information in written form or by email; they like to solve problems on their own.

Now suppose an extrovert wants to enlist the support of an introvert over a problem. The extrovert presents the problem to the introverted colleague but finds the person seemingly distant and unwilling to help. Conversely, the introvert feels that the extrovert is pushy and unwilling to give the introvert time to think things through.

If only the extrovert understood that the introvert isn't deliberately being unhelpful but simply finds it difficult to make decisions on the spot. If only the introvert could see that the extrovert isn't intentionally pushy but simply prefers to talk issues through. Recognizing their different personality preferences could help the two of them to understand each other and work together more effectively.

Take another example. A manager who is highly conscientious may want to plan out a project in meticulous detail while another who is less conscientious may just want to get on with it. You can imagine the frustrations that could cause them both.

There are of course other facets of personality (see Q67). But the point is this: What you value in yourself may drive others to distraction, and vice versa.

Our personalities are pretty much fixed by our genes – it's an accident of birth like being born left- or right-handed. You can force someone to write with their non-preferred hand, but it feels uncomfortable to them and it doesn't produce a very good result because you can't expect people to change who they are. As such, it is often easier to change your behavior to accommodate the preferences of others than try to change their behavior to accommodate yours. Rather than shout and scream or beg and plead with others to change how they are, change how you behave towards them – you'll save yourself a big headache and achieve better results too.

> What you value in yourself may drive others to distraction, and vice versa.

67 What are the major differences in people's personalities?

While typologies such as the Myers-Briggs Type Indicator (MBTI) have been popular for many years, modern psychology has since moved on. Twenty-first century psychologists generally agree that personality can be measured along five different dimensions, which can be summed up by the OCEAN acronym. To work effectively with others, take their preferences into account:

Openness to experience - "a person's need to seek new intellectual stimulation"

People who are high on openness to experience tend to be seen by …		People who are low on openness to experience tend to be seen by …	
… themselves and others who are high on this dimension as:	… people who are low on this dimension as:	… themselves and others who are low on this dimension as:	… people who are high on this dimension as:
Imaginative, open-minded, strategic, quick-witted	Idealistic, impractical, having only superficial interests, poor with detail	Down-to-earth, pragmatic, sensible, good with detail	Boring, narrow in outlook, close-minded, unimaginative

Conscientiousness - "a person's need to be responsible, structured and organized in how they live their lives"

People who are high on conscientiousness tend to be seen by …		People who are low on conscientiousness tend to be seen by …	
… themselves and others who are high on this dimension as:	… people who are low on this dimension as:	… themselves and others who are low on this dimension as:	… people who are high on this dimension as:
Organized, reliable, dependable, responsible	Inflexible, perfectionist, stubborn, slow to change	Spontaneous, flexible, easy-going, open-minded	Disorganized, unreliable, careless, impulsive

Extraversion - "a person's need for social interaction with other people"

People who are high on extraversion tend to be seen by …		People who are low on extraversion tend to be seen by …	
… themselves and others who are high on this dimension as:	… people who are low on extraversion as:	… themselves and others who are low on this dimension as:	… people who are high on extraversion as:
Sociable, outgoing, chatty, approachable	Flighty, easily distractible, loud, attention-seeking	Reserved, independent, considerate, good listeners	Quiet, distant, unapproachable, unfriendly

As you can see, people at either end of each dimension tend to see each other in very different ways.

Agreeableness - "a person's need to seek harmony and avoid conflict with others"

People who are high on agreeableness tend to be seen by …		People who are low on agreeableness tend to be seen by …	
… themselves and others who are high on this dimension as:	… people who are low on agreeableness as:	… themselves and others who are low on this dimension as:	… people who are high on agreeableness as:
Trusting, tactful, considerate, diplomatic	Two-faced, gullible, afraid of confrontation, cowardly	Straight-talking, forthright, direct, willing to "tell it as it is"	Blunt, insensitive, tactless, critical

Neuroticism - "a person's natural tendency to worry and be anxious"

People who are high on neuroticism tend to be seen by …		People who are low on neuroticism tend to be seen by …	
… themselves and others who are high on this dimension as:	… people who are low on neuroticism as:	… themselves and others who are low on this dimension as:	… people who are high on neuroticism as:
Sensitive to others' feelings, attentive, perceptive, self-aware	Nervous, anxious, tense, self-critical	Calm, self-confident, patient, even-tempered	Arrogant, aloof, emotionally impassive, indifferent to the feelings of others

For each of the five dimensions, work out whether you are high or low (or possibly medium). Then work out the traits of the people you encounter to work out where you may be clashing and how to alter your behavior to accommodate others better.

58 Why don't people listen to me?

People are illogical creatures who rarely respond to reason alone. Try as you might, you will not always succeed in changing someone's mind even with a broad-shouldered, square-jawed argument that outlines clear benefits for the team and wider organization.

Generally speaking, you can exert influence by either "pushing" or "pulling" people towards goals. You can push in a particular direction by telling them what to do, using authority or force of will, and making others feel that they *must* do as you say; you can pull in a direction by inspiring, exciting, and making others feel that they *want* to do as you say.

Not all people can be influenced, persuaded, or swayed in the same way. And even a single individual may respond to different styles of influence under different circumstances. The style of influence that is appropriate in an emergency may not be appropriate for a day-to-day meeting; what works in a negotiation with a customer may not work in seeking a favor from your boss. As such, the people who are the most successful at exerting influence flex their influencing style to accommodate both different individuals and different situations (see also Q20 on becoming an effective lobbyist).

Before attempting to influence anyone, start by appreciating where they stand on an issue by asking questions and listening to their thoughts and concerns (see Q65 on the active listening technique). I've mentioned it before but it's worth mentioning again: the likelihood of your success is strongly linked to both the quantity and quality of the questions you ask. Ask more questions and you are more likely to get at the nub of their issues. Once you have established their point of view, consider adapting your influencing style (see Q69) to meet the demands of the particular situation.

> Before attempting to influence anyone, start by appreciating where they stand on an issue.

59 How can I be more influential?

Generally speaking, if you want to be more influential, learn to soften your approach by pulling rather than pushing people toward goals. Listed in order, from the most heavy-handed and "pushing" at the top to engaging and "pulling" at the bottom, consider the following seven styles of influencing:

✓ *Commanding.* Using authority or force of will to compel others to do what is necessary. This "push" style of influence is particularly appropriate during times of crisis when quick, decisive action without lengthy discussion is needed.

✓ *Convincing.* Using logical arguments, facts and figures, and pros and cons to argue the merits of a case. Convincing relies on being analytical, cool-headed, and thorough, to "prove" the benefits of doing something. Convincing focuses on what people *should* do as opposed to making them feel they *want* to do it.

✓ *Compromising.* Looking for a solution or outcome that at least partly meets the needs of all parties. Compromising means entering into a discussion with a solution in mind, but being ready to make concessions around it (e.g. when asking for a pay rise, Q8). It requires a pragmatic give-and-take approach and making trade-offs to gain movement from other parties.

✓ *Collaborating*. Working with other people to find a solution that meets the needs of all parties. Collaborating means seeking involvement from others early on (see also Q22) to craft a solution together rather than going to them with a solution you have already dreamt up.

✓ *Cajoling*. Using empathy, warmth, charm, your likeability, and perhaps a smattering of flattery to beg a favor or otherwise persuade others to do what you want.

✓ *Championing*. Modeling a behavior or activity to set a personal example. Leaders often talk about "walking the talk," i.e. doing what they say. Championing an idea by showing others what it looks like and demonstrating its benefits can sometimes allow others to see that it is easier and more useful than they initially thought.

✓ *Calling into action*. Speaking with passion about a topic and inspiring others into believing that they must act. This "pull" influencing style often relies on painting a vivid picture (a vision) of an attractive and exciting future, and appealing to people's nobler instincts.

Most of us have one or two dominant influencing styles. Truly influential people rely more on pulling styles than pushing styles, but recognize there may be times when dramatic changes of style are necessary. The next time you need to influence an individual or a group, which style are you going use?

70 How can I fend off an office bully?

Bullying in the workplace does not always take the form of shouting and overt aggression. Bullying can result from inaction as well as action – for example from having responsibilities removed or being excluded from meetings, training, or other activities. People can feel bullied when they are constantly criticized without just reason, or they are regularly made the butt of jokes.

Bullying is a frighteningly common reality of working life that is rarely given the attention it deserves. There are no simple solutions to it, but help yourself to survive bullying by ensuring that you:

✓ *Gather evidence.* The moment you feel harassed or maltreated, begin to keep a written record of events, dates, and times, plus a list of people who may have observed incidents or their consequences. If you have any physical evidence such as emails or memos, keep these in a safe place too.

✓ *Broach the subject with the bully.* The person who is bullying you may genuinely not realize that you're suffering as a result of their comments, actions, or inaction. Some so-called bullies are merely incompetent or ignorant as opposed to intentionally malicious. Occasionally, taking that person aside for a private discussion can help the individual concerned to see the grief caused to you and rectify the situation. (See also Q62 on dealing with interpersonal conflict.)

✓ *Ask for help.* If the bullying does not stop, speak confidentially to your boss. If you feel that it is your boss who is bullying you, approach the human resources department. If you work in a small organization without an HR department, seek the counsel of a third party such as your union, a lawyer, or the Citizen's Advice Bureau or other similar establishments who can mediate and deal with the situation.

✓ *Be careful in speaking about the situation.* Speak to a trusted colleague if you want a second opinion. But be very, very sure that you can trust the person not to gossip about it. And avoid talking about the situation even when asked about it by other members of the team, as they may then be forced to take sides. Can you be sure it's your side they would take?

✓ *Make it official.* If you have exhausted every other option, consider making a formal written complaint to someone higher up the organization. Go to your boss's boss's boss and pursue your case until you're happy.

Bullying can result from inaction as well as action.

71 How many hours a week do I need to work to succeed?

A colleague of mine jokes, "Life is tough and then you die." While the sentiment is rather hard-hitting, he has a point. Life is tough. If you want to reach the top, you may have to put your life outside of work on hold; if you want to spend quality time with family and friends, you may not get as far as those who are willing to work crazy hours. You can't have it all. To put it rather simplistically, do you *live* to *work* or *work* to *live*?

There are some careers that are particularly demanding – either because they are very highly paid, such as those in banking and finance, law, and other professional services, or because they are exciting or possibly glamorous, such as those in television, entertainment, or creative industries such as fashion and advertising. No matter how talented and politically savvy you may be, if everyone else is working 50, 70, or 82.75 hours a week, you probably won't be able to get away with much less. To what extent are you willing to do what is necessary to succeed in your work?

> # Anyone who works hard without knowing why is doomed to an unhappy life.

In some organizations there may also be the added complication of "face time," or the need to be *seen* to be working long hours because bosses implicitly equate long hours with productivity. I used to work for one such organization in which colleagues used to ask only half-jokingly, "Are you having a half day?" if you left at 6pm. If that's the culture of your organization, you may need to be seen by your colleagues and bosses.

If you decide that career success is your number one driving ambition, then put in the hours. If you decide that you have priorities more important than your work, then find the time for them by reducing your workload (see also Q72) or finding a new job. No one can tell you whether to work to live or live to work. But having a vision of what you want your life to be like will help you to decide the path to choose (see Q14 to Q17). Whichever you end up doing, make sure it is through choice and not mere circumstance. Anyone who works hard without knowing why is doomed to an unhappy life.

72 How can I improve my work–life balance?

Q71 made the argument about work–life (or should that be life–work) balance – and here's a simple yet effective exercise in five steps for analyzing how you spend your time and re-prioritizing what's important to you:

1. Draw a four by three grid and cross out the last box, like this:

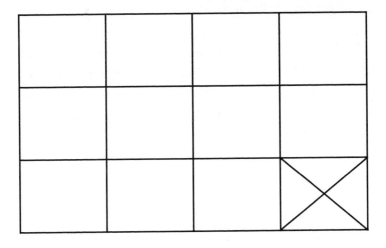

2. Fill in the boxes with how you spend your time. There are 168 hours in a week and we spend approximately 56 of these in bed. Which leaves us 112 hours to play with, so each of the 11 boxes represents approximately ten hours of our time. Consider an average week and write into each box a description of how you spent your time.

3. Start with the time you spend at work. If you work 40 hours a week, that's four boxes with the word "work" in them; 70 hours a week at work is seven boxes. A friend of mine is currently spending six hours a day commuting to his job on the other side of the city – so that's another three boxes every week.

4. Fill in the remaining boxes with time you spent on family, friends, your partner, children, your spirituality or faith, hobbies, leisure, exercise, housework, and so on. If you only spent five hours doing something that's half a box. But don't try to account for every single hour of every single day. We want to look at the main activities in which you invest time rather than the hour-by-hour detail.

5. Once you have finished allocating your time, consider how happy you are with the picture you have created. Consider how it compares with your vision of your perfect life (Q14).

Bear in mind that the number of boxes is fixed; you can't create more time, only use the time that you do have differently. If there is a discrepancy between how you spend your time and how you would like to spend it, ask yourself: What is holding you back from spending your time differently? And (perhaps by setting yourself SPORTY goals – Q17) how could you bring about the life you want to have?

73 How can I learn to say "no"?

Many people worry that turning down work or refusing requests presents a real risk to their careers. We all know that demonstrating a can-do attitude and a willingness to work hard can make us stand out for all the right reasons. But what people forget is that, while your boss's job is to stretch and challenge you, you must also give your boss feedback on how far and how fast you can be stretched by learning to say no occasionally. If you don't speak up, no one else is going to speak up for you.

It is always easier to turn down work if you have prepared good reasons for doing so. First identify your priorities and goals for each day (see Q28); then formulate responses for tactfully turning down requests that would otherwise derail you from achieving your goals for the day. Work out your reasons so that you don't need to scrabble around for an excuse on the spot. When a request comes your way, make sure to:

1. *Listen to the other person's request fully.* Nothing gets a person's back up more quickly than turning down his or her request when you've got only half the facts. Let the person speak without interruption to ensure you fully understand the individual's need. (see also Q65 on active listening).

2. *Explain why you are declining the request.* Provide your pre-prepared and hopefully compelling reason why you will not be

able to help with the person's request (see Q74 for different ways to say no). Perhaps you have more urgent or important tasks to complete; maybe you are not the best-placed person for the task, you have a personal commitment, or someone else has capacity to take it on instead.

3. *Reiterate your reasons.* Sometimes other people are too caught up in their own needs to really listen. Repeat your reasons politely, and do it two or three slightly different ways. If you believe that you have a genuine reason to turn down a request, go over it again rather than backing down the moment someone challenges you.

4. *But be prepared to compromise.* If the discussion seems to be going nowhere, think about concessions that you could make. If you can't work late this evening on a document, perhaps you'd be willing to look at their first draft in the morning. Or if you can't work on a project team, you might be willing to attend the kick-off meeting or commit other resources.

> # It is always easier to turn down work if you have prepared good reasons for doing so.

74 What are different ways I can say "no"?

Following on from Q73, no single method for saying "no" is going to work all of the time. Consider mixing up your approach for declining work:

1. *The direct no.* One approach would be to say no without giving a reason and leave it at that. Not perhaps the best tactic and it's listed here more to indicate what not to do.

2. *The reasoned no.* Explain your reason as to why you can't say yes. "I can't because ..." Remember that if you have worked out your priorities for your day or week, you are likely to have much stronger reasons for turning down other people's requests than if you must make up a reason on the spot.

3. *The empathetic no.* Show your appreciation of the other person's situation in an attempt to soften the blow of refusal, but ultimately say no. "I can see that you're swamped by work, but I have to say no because..."

4. *The alternative no.* Say no but offer an alternative of how you (or someone else) might be able to help. Rather than simply saying "no," you are saying "no, but..." for example, "I can't do it now, but I know I have time after my 2 o'clock

meeting" or "I don't think I'm the right person, but have you tried …?"

5. *The escalating no.* Rather than suggesting just the one option, keep escalating what you are prepared to do until you reach a compromise that works. Consider "I can't, but what if I came in an hour earlier tomorrow?" followed by "What if I promised that I would have a look at it tonight when I get home?" then "What if I have a quick look – but only for ten minutes right now?"

6. *The strait no.* Offer the other person a strait (i.e. rigid) choice between two options. This is not an escalating no in which you are offering to come to a compromise. Often a useful tactic with your boss, you are saying that you can only do one task or another – but not both. "I'd be happy to do that, but I already have the client proposal to do by lunchtime tomorrow. Which would you rather I get done?"

No single method will help you to escape every single request. But try different tactics on those occasions when you really do need to focus on your own priorities – whether they are to do with your work or just getting out of the office on time.

5 Do I need to build my profile at work?

If you want to climb the career ladder, possibly the most important advice to remember is: Achievements that go unnoticed by the right people (i.e. the big bosses who decide pay rises, bonuses, and promotions) may as well not exist.

You may be one of the many people who would rather let their achievements speak for themselves. However, remember that achievements do not speak. It is people who speak; achievements simply exist and often go unnoticed.

Self-marketing through building a profile and raising your visibility is a necessary part of climbing the career ladder. It makes the difference between a job well done and the job that gets you the promotion.

Many organizations talk about how they aim to be meritocratic but the reality is often tough to achieve. Decisions about promotions and pay are made by people, not all-seeing, all-knowing robots. And no matter how fair they may want to be, bosses can only make decisions based on what they know. If they don't know about that stellar piece of work you did, you will not receive the rewards you deserve.

> # Achievements that go unnoticed by the right people may as well not exist.

I once worked with a bank on a project called the Senior Development Review, which was aimed at identifying managers who should be fast-tracked in their careers. At a number of meetings, a director, the director's boss, and I discussed the fates of dozens of managers at a time. My job was to argue the merits of the managers, all of whom I had met. As you can imagine though, the managers who were known to the director and the director's boss got much better ratings and evaluations than those who were less well known.

The old adage says it's who you know, not what you know. Nowadays, it's who you know *and* what you know; the "what you know" bit allows you to do a good job, but the "who you know" bit ensures it gets noticed. Being good at your job needs to go hand-in-hand with building your profile.

Having a network (Q47) is a good starting point for building your profile. But the next step is to make sure you communicate your achievements.

76 How can I develop my profile and visibility at work?

Profile building is about communicating your successes and making yourself known. It's not about boasting and promoting your interests above those of everyone else. Here are some essential tips for developing your profile effectively:

✓ *Volunteer to work on projects outside of your day-to-day job.* Not all organizational problems and opportunities fall neatly under the remit of existing teams. Most organizations are full of projects and initiatives aimed at getting different departments to work together to achieve broader organizational goals. As most employees dislike moving out of their comfort zones, volunteering for such efforts can get you good exposure to more senior managers. Look for opportunities to join groups such as task forces, special working parties, cross-disciplinary teams, change projects, and so on.

✓ *Ask your boss for help.* Explain that you think you have more to offer the organization and take his or her advice on the projects and opportunities you should be pursuing to forge ahead.

✓ *Share genuinely good ideas.* Spend time before every meeting you attend thinking about ideas to share that could help others do their jobs better. Be careful about talking up your own successes – that's clearly self-interested promotion. Look instead to highlight processes, procedures, or techniques you may have developed; share tips about what works and lessons you have learned from your own mistakes. Think also about insight into your customers, rumors about competitors, best practices from other industries, and any other information you could share that both benefits others and demonstrates your brainpower.

✓ *Enhance your boss's reputation in front of senior people.* If you have a chance to talk about your work in front of high-ranking people, acknowledge explicitly your boss's role in guiding you. Your boss is hardly going to complain if you make him or her look good. And it makes you appear more modest by not trying to claim all of the credit.

In building your profile, remember the critical difference between communicating successes and empty boasting. Talking up your own successes makes you a vainglorious show-off; sharing useful ideas makes you someone to keep around.

> # Be careful about talking up your own successes – that's clearly self-interested promotion.

7 Can jargon ever be a force for good?

We all have a "jargon footprint" – how big is yours? Jargon can at once repel some people and draw others closer to you. As such, it would be foolish to say that all jargon is automatically bad.

Customers, for example, may not care about the technical features of a product; they are more usually interested only in its benefits. However, jargon can often be necessary if everyone in your own team uses it everyday.

If your bosses talk about "disambiguating" (ironically, a word meaning to "make clear") or "taking it offline" (discussing an issue in private) or not having the "bandwidth" (capacity) to deal with a problem, then you do too. If your organization has specific TLAs (three-letter acronyms) that people use, then you JDI (just do it) or JFDI (you can probably guess that one).

Use of jargon is often a cultural marker (see Q5) that signals whether you fit in or not. Just be careful to note how much of it is used around you. A particular trap is to carry buzzwords and techno-speak from one organization to the next – what was appropriate in your last organization could make you a joke in another.

A notable exception is the language of finance. While many managers may throw around terms such as ROI (return on investment) or CAGR (compound annual growth rate) or EBITDA (earnings before interest, tax, depreciation, and amortization), they don't always know what they mean or how to use them. Increasingly, bosses look to promote individuals who know how to achieve organizational goals – and even if your organization is not solely focused on profit, you can still be sure that it worries about cost. Money matters, and people who can understand at least the basic workings of finance put themselves in a much stronger position to be promoted. So befriend a finance manager in your organization today. They're not a bad sort. And imagine the difference it could make to your career if you could get to grips with the financial jargon that matters.

> What was appropriate in your last organization could make you a joke in another.

8 What is good meeting etiquette these days?

I read one survey in which 91 percent of employees confessed to having daydreamed in meetings. But I can hardly say that I'm surprised. We all spend so much time in meetings, meetings, and more meetings. Here are some tips for handling yours effectively:

✓ *Work out an agenda.* Whether you were asked to lead the meeting or not, remember that you're on display. Meetings are an opportunity for you to show others how smart and switched-on you are. If someone else is leading the meeting and loses his or her way, you can speak up and get the meeting back on track.

✓ *Use the clock to keep people in line.* Refer to the time as a way of hurrying people through the meeting if they dawdle unnecessarily. Once you have asked when people need to leave the meeting, you can make comments such as: "I'm conscious that we've only got another 15 minutes before Alex and Chris need to get away. Can I suggest we move on to discussing..."

✓ *Go with the flow.* If someone has said something positive, build on his or her comment by pointing out a different positive point. If someone has pointed out a flaw in the argument, that's the time to voice your concern. Look for the right point during the discussion to raise either positive or negative points.

✓ *Ask questions instead of being negative.* Avoid passing judgment on whether you think an idea is good or not. Contradicting someone by saying, "that won't work" implies you know better than anyone else in the room (see also Q9 on speaking your mind). Instead of pointing out a problem, acknowledge the other person's contribution and ask a question that invites others to seek a solution. If the team has no budget, rather than pointing it out, ask: "That's a great idea. How could we get the funding together for that?" Asking questions shows that you are can-do and solution-focused rather than can't-do and problem-focused.

✓ *Do what others do.* I worked in one organization in which we used to "flip" everything – a colleague was always keen to write agendas and capture thoughts on flipcharts. In another organization, people used to sit on desks or bean bags, stand or even sit cross-legged on the floor. If everyone in your team behaves a certain way, e.g. they like written agendas, don't spring up to the whiteboard.

> # Saying, "that won't work" implies you know better than anyone else in the room.

9 Why am I bored with my job?

Many of us experience that "Monday morning feeling" of not wanting to go to work. There can be many reasons why people may feel frustrated or anxious about their jobs (Q10). But the biggest reason for boredom is that you no longer enjoy – or perhaps never enjoyed – the tasks and activities you do from day to day. To identify what you could be doing to feel more motivated or even passionate, work your way through the following steps:

1. *Look at how you currently spend your time.* Estimate to the nearest hour how long you spend on different activities in a typical week. Take the average of several weeks and consider all of your activities, e.g. generating new ideas, analyzing data, selling to clients, solving problems, writing reports, coaching others, and so on.

2. *Look at which activities you most enjoyed doing.* Review your list of activities and identify the ones you find most enjoyable. What proportion of your week do you spend doing activities that you genuinely enjoy? (See Q80 for ways to change the nature of your work).

3. *Identify any gaps.* We all feel most intrinsically motivated when we are able to deploy our strengths. Consider whether you possess any strengths that you do not currently get a chance to use in your current job (see Q37, Q38 to identify your

strengths). For example, if you love working with children or speaking in public but don't currently have the opportunities to do so, add these to your list of favorite activities.

4. *Identify your longer-term goals.* We can sometimes force ourselves to stay motivated on an unpleasant task in the short-term if we know that it helps us to further our longer-term goals. For example, if you dislike dealing with financial matters but realize you need to develop at least an adequate level of financial awareness to achieve your longer-term goal of becoming a senior manager, you are more likely to persist with it than if you have no such ambition.

To be (bored) or not to be (bored), that is the question. What's your answer?

30 Is it possible to feel more passionate about my job?

You can't change how you feel about your job unless you change job or at least change parts of your job.

Of course you may feel that everyone gets that "Monday morning feeling" and that it's not that big a deal to feel passionate about your work. But ask yourself this: Would you be happy to continue doing your current job *for the rest of your working life?* If not, consider some of the following options:

✓ *Talking to your boss.* Approach your boss and explain that while you enjoy your job you think you could offer more to the organization by adjusting your duties and responsibilities. Bear in mind that many bosses are unsympathetic to what you want, but may be more inclined to listen if you can explain how such changes would help them. Phrase your request in terms of how changing your duties would not only make you happier but also more productive and therefore able to achieve organizational goals (see also Q68 and Q69 on exerting influence on others).

✓ *Moving into a new role within the organization.* If your boss is unwilling or unable to change your duties, consider seeking a role elsewhere within the organization. It's frequently easier to move into a new role with your existing employer than to pursue a new role with a new employer. Use your internal network (Q47) to investigate job openings or even particular project opportunities. Again, consider how you position your request. Talking to a new prospective boss about why you want to join his or her team is so much more compelling than talking about why you want to get away from another one.

✓ *Exploring options outside of the organization.* If your boss and organization are unwilling or unable to help, consider talking to people in your external network (Q51) to gather suggestions on career choices you could pursue (see also Q83 on changing careers).

Would you be happy to continue doing your current job for the *rest of your working life?*

31 How can I be happier in an existing job?

Perhaps you have reasons why you can't or won't leave your job. Whatever the case, consider some research done by The Gallup Organization, which found that 12 statements are highly correlated with feelings of motivation and engagement with work. These statements are as follows:

1. I know what is expected of me at work.

2. I have the materials and equipment I need to do my work right.

3. At work, I have the opportunity to do what I do best every day.

4. In the last seven days, I have received recognition or praise for doing good work.

5. My supervisor, or someone at work, seems to care about me as a person.

6. There is someone at work who encourages my development.

7. At work, my opinions seem to count.

8. The mission or purpose of my company makes me feel my job is important.

9. My associates or fellow employees are committed to doing quality work.

10. I have a best friend at work.

11. In the last six months, someone at work has talked to me about my progress.

12. This last year, I have had opportunities at work to learn and grow.

> # You *can* take control of your working environment.

At a glance, you may think that none of these statements is at all surprising. Again, as with so much in the world of work, the challenge is not in understanding them, but shaping your work environment to your needs.

Let's consider statement number 1. Even if you have a buffoon for a boss, look for ways in which you can take control. Ask your boss for precise expectations and learn to draw good instructions from him or her even if your boss doesn't do it naturally (see also Q91). How about the second statement? If you don't feel that you have the materials and equipment you need, ask for them. If no one will give you what you need, put a business case together that shows how having the right gear would allow you to become more productive. Number 11 looks at your progress – if someone isn't talking to you about it, why not proactively seek out the opportunity to do so? You get the idea hopefully.

The point is this: You *can* take control of your working environment. It may take months of concerted effort and it won't all happen at once. But if others are not giving you what you need, make a plan to get it anyway.

82 How can I find my calling in life?

Perhaps you have decided (for example by working through the options in Q80) that what you are currently doing in your job is not what you want to be doing forever.

Many people contemplating career changes try to find their calling in life, the one path that would make them feel motivated, inspired, passionate, and excited every day. But there's good news as well as bad.

First the bad news. I'm afraid there may not be a single path that will lead you to ultimate career and life fulfillment. However, the good news is that there may actually be *several* paths that could lead you to professional reinvention and career contentment.

Let's understand why. Suppose you identify you have four key strengths, let's call them A, B, C, and D, that you would love to deploy in your work on a daily basis. Perhaps you find a job that allows you to utilize strengths A, B, and D – but pursuing it might mean having to move to a new town. Maybe you find a new career that allows you to utilize strengths B, C, and D – but that one might mean having to study for qualifications that could take a few years. Another job may allow you to use only skills A and C – but perhaps that one pays quite a bit more.

Seek out experiences that let you try before you buy.

Searching for your one true calling in life may be a futile pursuit. Sure, there may be a *few* people who find jobs that allow them to utilize all of their key strengths every single day and earn enough for themselves and their families to live the lives they desire. But that can be difficult for the rest of us. We may not be able to find our "one true selves." Often, we may have *several possible* selves, each of which could make us happier. There may be no job in existence that allows you to utilize all of your strengths. Or you may have constraints that prevent you from achieving it for the time being.

As such, consider that the best way to make a career change is to seek out those *possible* selves. Seek out experiences that let you try before you buy. Dip your toe in the water, experiment, and flirt with possibilities before you choose what may be right for you (Q83).

83 What's the best way to explore new career options?

A good start is to identify your strengths so you know how you would like to be spending your time (see Q79). Even if you don't know what kinds of jobs would allow you to spend your time in those ways, it's a start. Then consider these suggestions in finding a new career:

✓ *Brainstorm possible jobs with people in your network.* Tell people you know that you're looking for a new job – possibly or even probably one that has nothing to do with what you've been doing so far. Just because you've been in law or marketing or retail doesn't mean you couldn't enter the wine trade, publishing, or children's entertainment. Let others know of your strengths and see if they can come up with ideas of job titles that could allow you to exercise those strengths – encourage them to come up with ideas no matter how crazy they might at first seem. It's often the so-called "silly" ideas that lead onto more viable ones.

✓ *Talk to strangers.* Canny networkers make use of what are known as "weak ties" – people who are not their first point of contact – to grow their networks indefinitely. The greater the diversity of people you talk to about possible career options, the greater your chances of stumbling on a great idea. A major advantage of talking to people who don't know you is that they have no preconceptions about you. Strangers can often see truths about us and come up with ideas that people who are closer to us may dismiss out of hand.

✓ *Seek opportunities to try out possible careers.* Once you develop ideas of new careers, try them out. Rather than pursuing the high-risk strategy of quitting your job to fling yourself headlong into a new career, look instead to sample possible career paths on a small scale. Use evenings and weekends and extended holidays to moonlight and dabble through freelance assignments, short courses, and part-time jobs. Ask whether you can shadow someone and observe what the work is like or volunteer to work for free. Test out different career options without jeopardizing what you are currently doing. When you find yourself bubbling over with excitement in the work you try out, you'll know that's the right option for you.

> # Try out possible career paths on a small scale.

84 I want a new job – how can I write a great CV and pass interviews?

Looking for a new job is a massive topic, but here are some top tips for landing your next job:

✓ *Use your network.* Job hunters often waste hours searching the Web for jobs and applying for advertised positions. However, experts estimate that between 50 and 85 percent of all positions are filled by word of mouth – through employee recommendations, referrals from trusted associates, tip-offs, and direct contact. Whether you are looking for a new job or an entirely new career, the more people you can tell about the work you want, the more they will be able to keep an eye out for possible opportunities.

✓ *Research employers to speak to.* Employers like to feel that you want to work for their organization as opposed to just any organization. Make sure you read their marketing literature, visit their website, and even drop by their shops, branches, salons, or whatever other physical locations you can call on to be able to talk about and demonstrate how much you want to work for any given organization.

✓ *Tailor your CV.* It used to be traditional to have one CV that you could send to every employer. Unfortunately, those times have passed. Candidates are working harder to impress employers, and the advent of the personal computer means that everyone can tweak and tinker with their CVs. Make sure you arrange the achievements on your CV and paraphrase key skills to mirror the precise requirements of each job.

✓ *Think about chemistry and competence.* Employers of course look for competent candidates. But they also want to hire people they like. In addition to preparing your answers to likely interview questions, aim to control your body language and tone of voice to project your personality, enthusiasm, and an appropriate sense of humor. Be a real person, not just a business person.

✓ *Buy Rob Yeung's other book.* The book *Should I Tell the Truth? And 99 Other Questions about Succeeding at Interviews and Job Hunting* is also published by the lovely folk at Cyan Books. I'm afraid job hunting really is too vast a topic to be able to do it justice here. But trust me, if you want to understand the tricks and techniques that will get you that job, buy the book!

85 How can I achieve fulfillment in my working life?

Being truly fulfilled at work comes not only from considering what you put into your work, but also what you get out of it.

I've already mentioned that finding a great job means finding work that allows you to exercise more of your strengths on a daily basis (Q36). But that's only half of the equation. The other half of the equation, and the difference between a great job and a perfect one, is in knowing that your work is also achieving outcomes that you find important.

Let's take an example. Suppose you discover that you have three key strengths: communicating with people face-to-face, working within a small team, and managing projects from start to finish. But consider the exceptionally broad range of outcomes that you could realize in exercising those three strengths. For example, you could work in a small consultancy that helps entrepreneurs to grow their businesses. You could work in a tight-knit team that is perhaps part of a larger organization that helps IT directors to manage change effectively. You might feel that the greatest buzz comes from working with three or four like-minded individuals to teach language skills to refugees who have been displaced from their native countries. The list is endless: working with children who have suffered the loss of a parent, pet owners who have sick animals, middle managers who need to lose weight, low-income families looking for inexpensive housing, and so on. All of those jobs would allow you to deploy your three key strengths but, as you can see, achieve very different outcomes.

You get the idea. Outcomes are important too. While deploying your signature strengths will allow you to enjoy your time and feel time fly by quickly, it is only by identifying the kinds of results you want to achieve that will help you to feel as fulfilled as humanly possible in your work. So what kind of outcomes are important to you?

86 How can I become an entrepreneur?

More and more people aspire to set up their own businesses, ranging from people offering their services part-time from home-based offices to those seeking tens of millions in funding to build international empires.

You may have heard stories of entrepreneurs who, despite being ordinary people, without money or contacts, came together in an empty garage and built extraordinary businesses. But dig deeper and you will find that such tales are usually media myths – trust me, I did dig deeper into some of the more popular ones. The truth is that canny entrepreneurs are not just folk who threw their jobs in and triumphed in the face of overwhelming odds; smart entrepreneurs plan and build up towards setting up their own ventures. If you want to launch yourself as an entrepreneur, be sure to:

✓ *Identify the skills and know-how you need.* Map out what your role in any future venture might look like. Do you want to be the owner of your own small business, managing director of a larger venture, head of technology, human resources director or something else? Once you have identified the vision of what you would like to achieve (Q14), work out the skills, qualifications, and knowledge you must acquire to succeed in that role.

✓ *Plug the gaps.* Pursue opportunities to acquire the right skills by persuading senior folk to let you work on the right projects or attend relevant courses – keep quiet about your true motives though and always explain how such opportunities would help you to further organizational goals instead. Once you have exhausted whatever a current organization can do for you, look to move on to a new one.

✓ *Network systematically.* Another persistent myth is of the lone entrepreneur, working single-handedly against the odds. The reality is that successful entrepreneurs draw upon vast networks of contacts for advice, information, assistance, and funding. Make it a goal of yours to extend and maintain your network (Q51, Q52).

✓ *Find ways to compensate for your weaknesses.* No one is good at everything. If the finances don't come easily to you, buy some software that will allow you to do it, hire a good accountant, or find a business partner who will look after the numbers. If you're good with implementation but not so hot on ideas, look for someone who is a font of creativity and imagination (see also Q35).

> # Smart entrepreneurs plan and build up towards setting up their own ventures.

87 Do I really need a mentor?

Mentors are possibly one of the best-kept secrets of career success. Why try to succeed on your own when someone who has seen and done it all can guide you? So the answer to the question is: Yes you need a mentor. Because having one will help you to succeed.

Mentors can tell you the secret rules of the workplace and counsel you on avoiding gaffes that others have committed. They can act as a sounding board for day-to-day operational issues or act as a more strategic resource in talking about the direction and progress of your career. They can offer feedback on how you are perceived and may even furnish you with introductions to other important people within the organization who can help you in your career. They can speak up in senior discussions, recommending you for opportunities or perhaps defending you too.

You can have more than one mentor too. If you are just starting out in your career, a mentor who is perhaps only a few years more senior than you might be able to guide you through some of the challenges you face on a day-to-day basis. A mentor who is much more senior may be able to focus on the broader perspective. Perhaps a mentor within another organization could act as a sounding board if you have goals that will eventually require you to leave a current organization.

If you're wondering why anyone would want to be your sounding board and advisor, the simple truth is that mentors get something

You need a mentor because having one will help you to succeed.

out of it too. Perhaps they get an emotional payback from making a contribution, passing their knowledge on, and creating a legacy. Perhaps some find it flattering or feel like proud parents in helping someone to grow and succeed. In same cases, their goals may be much more tangible, in using you as a gopher for minor projects and pieces of work.

A mentor is invaluable if you want to succeed – Luke Skywalker would never have defeated the evil empire without good old Yoda. However, mentoring relationships do not simply happen. Even if an organization has a formal mentoring scheme, you are not guaranteed that your mentor will be any good or that the two of you will have sufficient chemistry for it to work properly. Guess whose job it is to find a good mentor?

88 How can I find my Yoda?

If you sit around hoping for a mentor to "adopt" you, you might get lucky. But, then again, you might not. If you have goals and ambitions to succeed in your career, I would strongly urge you to take charge and find your own mentor. Okay, maybe you won't find your own short, wrinkly, green-skinned Jedi master, but consider these guidelines in identifying and approaching potential mentors:

✓ *Identify potential mentors.* The most useful mentors are those who are both respected and in a position of influence. Seniority is of little use if other managers do not value their views. Qualities such as credibility and integrity can't be overlooked in choosing a mentor. Begin your search for a mentor by building your network and looking for suitable candidates.

✓ *Get in front of potential mentors.* If a potential mentor is only a few years ahead of you along the career path, you could simply ask the person if he or she would consider mentoring you. However, if your would-be mentor is considerably more senior, he or she may find it impertinent that you – a nobody in the lower reaches of the organization – should dare ask him or her to mentor you. Your approach may need to be more subtle, by demonstrating your skills and credibility to your potential mentor by working for or alongside that person. Look at the individual's current projects and ask whether you can help in some way. Explain that you are keen to take on work to develop your skills and experience and then deliver results. You won't impress senior mentors unless you can first demonstrate you have the attitude, skills and qualities that set you above the rest of your colleagues.

✓ *Look for chemistry.* There is no point asking someone to mentor you if you feel awkward around that person. Likewise, you will not get much out of a mentor if he or she struggles to warm to you.

✓ *Frame your request in positive terms.* Approach your mentor once you have proven your worth through a project or piece of work and explain that you would value his or her occasional guidance as your mentor. Position your request not only in terms of what you want, but also what you can do for the organization to avoid coming across as too self-interested.

✓ *Treat your mentor as a prized resource.* Avoid bothering your mentor with trivial matters. Use time with your mentor to talk about strategic issues and key decisions. Remember that it's your responsibility to steer the meetings, so prepare assiduously to make the best of your meetings together.

89 How can I solve (or avert) a mid-life (or quarter-life) crisis?

It used to be the case that mainly 40-something-year-old men used to experience mid-life crises. Increasingly, it's both men and women in their thirties and even twenties who are starting to question their purposes in life – so much so that it's even been dubbed the quarter-life crisis.

The traditional model of success holds that, if life is a game, "winning" is defined by having more money, responsibility, power, and status. Unfortunately, surveys show that people are working increasingly longer hours and earning only greater job dissatisfaction and the symptoms of burnout. Too many people are sacrificing their personal desires, putting up with being only moderately happy, and even pretending to enjoy their work, in order to succeed.

You only have one life. How will you live yours? Consider that a well-adjusted life should comprise a balance between three aspects of "winning":

✓ *Success.* Most of us know what traditional success looks like – achieving more, striving to accomplish ever-greater goals, earning more, possessing more, consuming more. Traditional success is really about salary and status.

✓ *Satisfaction.* Think of the gratification, enjoyment, feelings of pleasure or contentment you get from what you do from moment to moment (see also Q82). Striving to earn more in order to build a comfortable retirement for yourself or a future for your family is a noble aim. But to what extent are you willing to sacrifice your own desires for a sense of enjoyment from your work? Don't think that your family will ever thank you for spending every hour at the office simply to put a roof over their heads.

✓ *Significance.* People will never remember you for your expensive clothes or your flashy car. But you can leave a legacy that will have a positive impact on people you care about. Creating a way to help others – whether it's your immediate family or friends, local community or people in the wider world – often helps many people to experience a sense of fulfillment that cannot always be gained from acquiring material toys.

There is no right answer as to what your life should look like. There are those in life who thrive by focusing solely on financial and material success. But so too are there many people who need a greater balance between success, satisfaction, and significance. To solve or avoid any crisis, consider what unique combination of the three you need in your life.

> # You only have one life. How will you live yours?

90 Are copying and stealing really good tactics for career success?

In answer to this question, I can definitely say yes. Copying and stealing are thoroughly useful tactics for achieving career success. In fact, I would go so far as to say that refusing to copy and steal could potentially be fatal to your career.

But perhaps I should explain before you get the wrong idea. You should copy *people's behaviors* and steal *good ideas*. Organizational life positively thrives on copying and stealing. And here's how you can make these two tactics work for you in practice:

✓ *Copying people's behaviors.* Look around you for role models. Study people who have achieved the career and life you want. Interestingly, you may learn more from observing them than asking them; many top performers often don't realize or can't articulate what makes them different and more successful. Observe what they do or say and see what you can adapt and incorporate into your own behavioral repertoire. For example, suppose you don't naturally feel comfortable giving presentations or speaking in public, but if you find someone who has a way of using their voice to enthrall an audience, why not see if you can assimilate it into your style of presenting? Or if you spot a particularly charismatic manager with a certain way of greeting people that makes others relax and open up, why not adapt the mannerism? Seeking role models – as well as spotting the mistakes that anti-role models makes – can speed your progress towards promotion or whatever other goals you may have.

✓ *Stealing good ideas.* Why reinvent the wheel? Businesses rarely reinvent the wheel and, in fact, there's a whole industry that exists solely to steal ideas – it's called "competitive intelligence" or "benchmarking" or "best practice sharing." So look at the processes and procedures, tools and techniques that other people use. Look not only at your colleagues within other teams, but also your customers and competitors to identify ways of working that you could adopt for your own. Ethically, you have nothing to lose. Of course copying a colleague's idea, claiming you invented it, trying to pass it off as your own, and taking the credit would be very, very wrong. But tell your bosses that you got the inspiration for a new method from a competitor and they will probably be very, very delighted.

Copy and steal. Just make sure you copy only *behaviors* and steal only *ideas.*

Why reinvent the wheel?

91 How can I manage my useless and/or bastard boss?

Bad bosses can make our jobs feel like hell on earth, but the truth is that few bosses set out to be bad bosses. They're only human and probably struggling to cope with their useless and/or bastard bosses too. Manage your boss in the following ways:

✓ *Position requests in the context of your boss's objectives.* Ask your boss openly about his or her targets and objectives and look for ways to help your boss meet them. It's a cliché to speak of the "bigger picture," but helping bosses to achieve their goals makes them exceedingly grateful. Always state any requests in terms of how it will help the team and your boss rather than only how it will help you. Suppose a particular type of work bores you and you want to ask for more interesting work. Unfortunately, your boss will only be able to give you more interesting work if the boring work can be dealt with somehow. So find people elsewhere in the organization who could do the work better; or help your boss to design a new process that eliminates the boring work. That way both you and your boss benefit.

✓ *Establish explicit ground rules for effective working.* Much friction with bosses comes down to differences in individual style (see also Q68). Take the time to ask your boss how you should work with him or her. It's your responsibility to match your boss's style rather than the other way around. Does your boss prefer to give and receive briefings in person or in written form? Does your boss need to be kept in the loop on a moment-by-moment basis or want you to get on and work as independently as possible? Does your boss want a strictly professional relationship or more of a personal, friendly one too?

✓ *Explore implicit rules indirectly.* You may wish to explore certain rules not through direct discussion with your boss but through observation or discussion with other members of the team. Consider for example the extent to which your boss welcomes criticism or is amenable to new ideas.

Much of managing a boss is about understanding how to change your behavior to match their style rather than the other way around. You will rarely – if ever – have the opportunity to point out your boss's mistakes (although see Q58 on using praise and encouragement to reinforce good behavior and train your boss like a puppy).

> # Helping bosses to achieve their goals makes them exceedingly grateful.

92 Should I sleep with the boss?

People like having sex. And given that people spend somewhere between a handful to 100 hours at work every week, they inevitably want to have sex with someone from work (or even at work). In one survey, 35 percent of managers confessed to having had a fling with a colleague.

Romance at work is only slightly less dangerous than swimming through shark-infested waters with a shaving cut. But add in the complexities of a boss–subordinate relationship and it's like tossing naval mines into the waters too. Here are some thoughts on the matter:

✓ *Be very, very sure there is a mutual attraction.* British workers alone filed nearly 30,000 sexual discrimination complaints with tribunals last year. What you consider harmless flirting could be someone else's idea of harassment. If you happen to be someone's boss, that merely adds weight to their claim that you abused your authority.

✓ *Remember that almost no tryst with a colleague will boost your career in the long run.* Chances are the relationship will combust and cause you more trouble than it was worth. Or any benefit will be countered by your other colleagues' resentment toward you. And that's not even mentioning the fact you may be breaking your employer's policy on workplace romances and risking both your jobs.

✓ *Consider that the harm to your career is in direct proportion of how much the two of you have to work together.* Entering into a relationship with someone in another department may have few repercussions even if it ends badly. The same cannot be said if you work in the same team. Even worse if one of you is the boss.

✓ *Flirt with care.* Obviously mentioning a colleague's breasts is a clear red flag, but even relaying an ironic comment from the girls in the office about the post boy's "pert bottom" could land you in hot water. Your intentions are irrelevant; employment legislation is interested only in whether the target of your attentions feels harassed or not.

✓ *Bear in mind that colleagues will always find out about three months before you think they've found out.* Human beings have remarkably acute, albeit subconscious, systems for reading body language. Staggering your arrival and departure times will not protect you from gossip.

But if you're gonna do it, you're gonna do it. The least you can do is have fun...

93 How can I keep up with the changing world?

Time and again, you will hear management experts and business commentators bleat on about the quickening pace of change. And, for once, they're right. Change has been happening fast and will only accelerate in the coming years. But what can you do about it?

Here are some pointers for helping yourself to keep up with developments in the wider world:

✓ *Network outside of your comfort zone.* Go to the same meetings and conferences and you will keep meeting the same people. Set yourself a target – whether you can only manage it once a year or once a month – to visit a forum you would not normally have contact with. Collect business cards and focus on forging some quality relationships.

✓ *Ask questions.* Don't be afraid to look stupid. It's braver to ask "why?" than to pretend (like everyone else) that you understand what's going on.

✓ *Explore technology.* Especially if your job has little or nothing to do with IT, make it your duty to trawl the web, learn about innovations in fields ranging from pharmaceuticals and physics to car design and online developments.

✓ *Read eclectically.* Avoid reading only the same trade and business publications. Of course it's notable that you read at all, but do it more widely. Once a month, buy a stack of magazines you have never read before and read them with a view to extracting a handful of insights or applications that you can use in your work. When you meet someone you respect, ask them about the best book they read recently; buy it, read it, then get in touch with the person to share your thoughts. Oh, and you've just managed to add another person to your network too.

✓ *Make time to create and innovate.* Invest time discussing new ideas with like-minded, but cross-disciplinary individuals. You may need to assemble such a group yourself. Perhaps ask a volunteer each time to give a short presentation on a topic. Doesn't matter what the topic is so long as it is new, different, and fresh to the other people in the room. Such sessions may spark further ideas that could be applicable to your own field.

It's braver to ask "why?" than to pretend (like everyone else) that you understand what's going on.

---

94 So what's all this rubbish about having a personal brand?

Brands are big business. Tell the time with a Tag Heuer or a Swatch, carry Louis Vuitton or Samsonite luggage, wear Dolce & Gabbana or Abercrombie & Fitch – each brand brings to mind different qualities and attributes. And it's the same with you whether you like it or not.

Your colleagues have a certain perception of you – you have a brand. You may cringe at the idea of having one, but you have one nonetheless. Whether you actively manage it or not, people have a particular impression of you. And how they treat you and what they say about you to others is based on that perception, and not how you really are.

Perception trumps reality every time. Doesn't matter if you think of yourself as reserved and hard-working if others think you're arrogant. Doesn't matter if you think of yourself as confident and forthright if your colleagues see you as a bit of a wallflower.

Granddaddy uber-guru Tom Peters was the first commentator to point out that, in an age in which we can no longer assume jobs for life, we are increasingly becoming CEOs and the boards of our own personal companies (see also Q12). As such, consider what the marketing director part of you has to say about your personal brand.

> # Discover what you are known for; then figure out what you would *like* to be known for.

The first step is to carry out some market research. Quiz your colleagues for candid feedback on how they see you. Ask about your distinguishing qualities (both bad and good). Ask them to describe in only three words your strengths and what they value you for, and another three words for your flaws and what they can feel frustrated by. Ask them to cast their minds back to their first impressions of you to tell you exactly what they thought of you. Ask your boss, customers, and even close friends – anyone who you trust to give you the unvarnished truth.

You may not like what you hear, but at least you will know for certain. Your personal brand can help or hinder your career, but you can't understand which until you know how you are currently perceived. Discover what you are known for; then figure out what you would *like* to be known for.

95 How can I create or revamp my personal brand?

Once you've understood how you are currently perceived (Q94), you can work on adding further qualities to your brand. Decide on no more than three qualities, attributes, or traits that you would like others to associate with you to weave into your behavior.

Whether you are meeting new customers for the first time or dealing with long-standing colleagues, think about the image or impression you want to leave them with. If there could be only three qualities you want people to remember you for, what would they be?

I say only three because brands change slowly and only with great effort. People will only notice a trait of yours if they see it demonstrated again, again, and again. Trying to change more than three qualities about yourself at once will only dilute your message. Strong brands require focus, feedback on progress, and continuing efforts to keep them on track.

Think about the qualities you must demonstrate to achieve your career goals. If people tend to get promoted for demonstrating certain values, perhaps that gives you a clue about the qualities you want to convey. Or if your ultimate goal is to set up your own business and attract potential investors and customers to you, think about the different qualities you might need for that too.

Think about your choice of words, tone of voice, body language, and facial expressions. Think too about the impression you create through your clothes, your written and electronic correspondence, and even the voicemail greeting that callers hear when they can't reach you in person.

If you need to move from your technical/geek past towards a leader-like future, prepare clever questions to ask in meetings, wear a more expensive suit, learn to pause sagely before answering questions, and so on. If you want to recast yourself as a soul of diplomacy, learn to ask questions such as "what do other people think about...?" and "would it be right to say that...?" rather than making pronouncements such as "surely..." or "obviously..." If you need to rebrand yourself as someone who is optimistic, learn to bite your tongue, wear brighter colors, record yourself laughing on your voicemail, whatever works for you and your organization's culture.

So, what key qualities do you want to convey that will help you to get ahead?

People will only notice a trait of yours if they see it demonstrated again, again and again.

---

96 What's the best way to handle a crisis at work?

When we face a crisis, whether it's a sudden emergency or a major problem that has been looming for some time, we often let our emotions take over. Perhaps we want to get angry or run away, cry or become paralyzed into inaction – all of which gets in the way of handling it well.

The way to handle a crisis is to engage the rational processes of your brain. Whether you are facing a personal catastrophe or a team tragedy, think – not feel – your way through any situation by asking yourself the six STRAIN questions:

✓ *Scale.* How big a deal is this on a scale of 1 to 10? Psychologists have spotted that people often experience a phenomenon called catastrophic thinking – blowing things out of proportion – in a crisis. What's the worst that could happen? Will you get sent to prison, see your children taken away or have your house repossessed? Taking those events as 9s or 10s, how highly would your current crisis score?

✓ *Time.* How much of an issue will this be in six months' time? Often, what seemed awful yesterday turns out to be not so bad today. Consider how it might look if you left it for a few days, weeks, or months. Anything that is causing you a headache today might not be so calamitous in six months' time.

✓ *Response.* Has your response so far been appropriate and effective? Perhaps so far you have got angry, said, "I told you so," or tried to ignore the problem. Whatever you have tried, quizzing yourself about what you have said or done so far will stop you from behaving unproductively.

✓ *Actions.* What could you do to better the situation? What's done is done and it's time to focus on a solution going forwards. What could you do, who could you turn to or talk to, what are your options for action in either the next few minutes or next few months that would help you through the situation?

✓ *Implications.* What are the implications of this situation for your long-term goals or vision? We may hesitate to take action because we are worried or scared. But spending a few minutes reviewing our long-term goals or vision could inspire us into action.

✓ *Next time.* Once the dust has settled, ask yourself what you can learn from the situation. How could you deal with a similar situation next time or prevent it from happening in the first place?

Going through the discipline of these six questions will force you to think more rationally and choose the right actions to take. Never let yourself falter in a crisis again.

Are you going to get sent to prison, have your children taken away from you or your house repossessed?

7 How can I develop my charisma and presence?

Some people just have it. They command a room and demand respect. When they speak, others listen. It has been called gravitas, charisma, presence, or even star quality. If you want to stop people in their tracks and ascend within your organization, learn to behave in an increasingly leader-like fashion. Here's how to get it:

✓ *Eliminate verbal tics and phrases.* Most of us have one. Several years into my career, a colleague told me that I used the phrase "you know" a dozen times in a single meeting. I was mortified. Ask a colleague to dissect your language during meetings and inform you about "ums," "ers," or any other annoying speech habits.

✓ *Show respect for others.* Count the ratio of positive to negative comments you make and aim for your positive comments to outweigh negative comments by five to one.

✓ *Speak with conviction.* When expressing your opinion, avoid using words such as "hopefully," "maybe," or "probably." Such words weaken your position and send out unconscious messages that even you aren't convinced by your own arguments.

✓ *Lower your register.* While a higher pitch can be used to indicate enthusiasm or excitement, a lower pitch is more usually associated with gravitas and distinction.

✓ *Slow down and use pauses.* Nervousness causes many people to speak more quickly. Research shows that the adage "less is more" is particularly true when it comes to making an impact. If you struggle to communicate succinctly, invest time before important meetings deciding how you will get your points across in fewer words. Pausing momentarily before each sentence encourages others to pay more attention and helps eliminate verbal tics too.

✓ *Project your voice.* Whispering quietly like a mouse hardly bespeaks substance and weightiness. Quite simply, people with gravitas tend to be louder. Learn to breathe from your diaphragm (as professional singers do) to make your words almost imperceptibly louder than others in the room.

✓ *Punctuate your words with appropriate body language.* Research shows that people who gesture on key points tend to be rated by others as more impactful than those who either do not gesture or gesture all the time. Refine your approach to using your hands and body movement by observing role models (see also Q90 on observing others).

98 What's the difference between a manager and a leader?

It's been said that managers focus on doing things right, while leaders focus on doing the right things. If that doesn't make much sense, consider the following seven differences.

Managers	Leaders
✓ Rely on command and control "push" techniques – "do it my way."	✓ Rely on inspiration and engagement "pull" techniques – "let's do it!"
✓ Create plans of what needs doing.	✓ Create visions of what is possible.

Managers	Leaders
✓ Focus on following processes, procedures and rules - "let's do it how the organization tells us we need to do it (even if we don't get the right result)."	✓ Focus on outcomes and results - "let's do whatever it takes (even if it means bending some of the rules) to achieve the right result."
✓ Expect others to minimize risk and avoid making mistakes.	✓ Encourage others to experiment, take controlled risks, make occasional mistakes, and find better ways of working.
✓ Delegate by explaining to members of the team not only what they need to achieve, but also how to do it.	✓ Coach by explaining to members of the team what they need to achieve, but leave them to figure out how.
✓ Focus on getting tasks done.	✓ Focus on developing people.
✓ Try to change and develop members of the team to meet the needs of their roles.	✓ Try to change and develop roles to meet the needs of members of the team.

N.B. Aim to be a leader, not a mere manager.

99 How can I be a great leader?

Leadership is a vast topic that continues to fill many, many books. However, to save you from reading them all, I believe that there are a handful of key principles that will allow anyone with responsibility for managing others to become a good leader:

✓ *Identify, communicate, and live your values.* Spend some time identifying your values, what you believe is important and worth fighting for. Then share your values and periodically remind your team of them so they understand how you expect them to behave. And remember to behave in line with your own values too – a manager who tells others to behave in one way but behaves in another has zero credibility.

✓ *Create a shared vision.* Much in the same way as you (should hopefully) have developed your own vision (Q13), you need to work with your team to create jointly a vision for the team. Get their involvement in crafting an inspiring vision that shows each member of the team how achieving the aims of the organization will be good for them individually.

✓ *Ask questions, don't tell.* Whatever the objectives of the team, invite the members of your team to discuss how best to tackle them. A manager who apportions work to their team is implicitly saying, "I know what's best for you." A leader who asks, "how should we do this?" makes members of the team feel that they can genuinely contribute and have a say in how the team is run (see also Q69 on using "pull" rather than "push" methods of influence).

✓ *Tailor work to individual needs.* Figure out what excites each individual within your team and then give that person work that, as far as possible, meets those needs. It doesn't matter if the person is good at the task or not – the individual will get better with practice and coaching on your part to grow his or her confidence. If you can help your team to find work that they enjoy and can improve on, you will build loyalty and commitment from them. Poor managers often treat members of their teams as clones, giving everyone the same work and expecting them to be equally good and equally interested in everything; good leaders treat members of their teams as individuals, giving them different work that recognizes their individual strengths and levels of interest.

> # A manager who tells others to behave in one way but behaves in another has zero credibility.

Any final tips on creating a successful and fulfilling career?

This book has answered dozens of questions tackling matters specific and broad. Consider the following pointers a recap of the main themes for carving out a great career:

✓ *Think both big and small.* A vision is effectively a big, scary yet exhilarating, audacious yet achievable goal. Whatever your goals in life – whether you want to get to the very top or reduce the inconvenience that your work has on your life – you should start with a vision. So that's the big bit. But the small bit comes in breaking down your big goal into baby steps – small, easily attainable steps that you can take one day at a time. As the legendary Chinese proverb goes: "A journey of a thousand miles starts with a single step."

✓ *Make yourself eminently employable.* No one can guarantee that you will have a job for life so take control of your own career.

Make yourself redundancy-proof by developing your own portfolio of smoking-hot skills and kick-ass experiences. That way, if you need a new job – whether you've lost one or simply lost interest in it – you can jump straight into the next one.

✓ *Network as if your life depends upon it.* Build genuine relationships with people. If you are known and liked by lots of people, you will thrive.

✓ *Be a real person, not a businessperson.* High achievers rarely focus on their career above all else. Top career people use leisure and other activities outside of work as a pressure valve for the stresses of work. In any case, being able to talk only about your work is... yawn... boring, and not the way to win friends and influence people.

✓ *Work on your career as well as in it.* Set time aside regularly – perhaps both monthly and quarterly – to review your progress towards your vision and long-term goals. Reflect on your progress to cull activities that aren't working and invest in new activities to propel you towards your goals. Be ruthless in protecting the time to work on your career; avoid at all costs letting day-to-day concerns get in the way of your long-term aspirations.

I wish you great success and fulfillment in your life and career. And please do share your stories with me too.

Rob Yeung
rob@talentspace.co.uk

Take control of your own career.

About the Author – Dr Rob Yeung

As a psychologist and coach, Dr Rob Yeung helps other people to achieve their goals. He coaches people who want to climb the corporate ladder, be more fulfilled in their work, pursue new jobs, work to rebalance their work and home lives, or change career entirely.

Rob helps people one-on-one, in front of audiences of hundreds, on the Web, in print, and on television. As an international speaker, he inspires and informs, educates and entertains – addressing audiences spanning business leaders and entrepreneurs, front-line employees and back office staff. He helps through his books too, having written over a dozen books that tackle workplace issues from getting a new job to getting ahead. And he helps on television, as an expert on everything from CNN to *Big Brother*, and as the presenter of programmes including *How To Get Your Dream Job* for the BBC.

For more information, visit www.robyeung.com.

ALSO BY DR ROB YEUNG

Whatever you're looking for, this book tells you everything you need to know about finding the perfect job. Finding your next job is a game with its own set of rules. While other books teach you what rules to follow, this book tells you which ones to flex a bit or ignore entirely. *Should I Tell the Truth?* literally rewrites the rule book on job hunting.

This controversial book provides informative, easy-to-digest, and entertaining answers to 100 questions such as: What does the perfect CV look like? Is it worth sending speculative applications? What are interviewers *really* looking for? What are the chances of getting caught if I lie? Should I fake on personality tests?

Should I Tell the Truth? is about how to get hired. You'll find in this book the answers to the questions that you have always wanted to ask, as well as the answers to the questions that you *should* be asking. Get your next job now.

ISBN 978-0-462-09919-4 / £9.99